THE
GRANTBUILDER™

STEP-BY-STEP GUIDE TO
GRANT WRITING
WORKBOOK
2ND EDITION

www.anthuriumpublishing.com

LA QUETTA M. SHAMBLEE, M.B.A.

AN OFFICIAL PROFESSIONAL EDUCATION SERIES PUBLICATION OF
THE CENTER FOR GRANTWRITING

ANTHURIUM PUBLISHING LLC
710 South Myrtle Ave No. 293
Monrovia, California 91016
www.anthuriumpublishing.com

The Grantbuilder™: Step-by-Step Guide to Grant Writing
by La Quetta M. Shamblee, M.B.A.

A professional education publication of The Center for Grant Writing™

The Grantbuilder ™ and The Center for Grant Writing ™ and related trade dress are trademarks or registered trademarks of La Quetta M. Shamblee and/or affiliates in the United States and may not be used without written permission.

ISBN-13: 978-0-9897188-2-0

ISBN-10: 0-9897188-2-4

Cover design by Adrianne Marie Hall
Interior illustrations provided by Adrianne Marie Hall
Interior diagrams provided by La Quetta M. Shamblee.

Limit of Liability and Disclaimer of Warranty:

The information contained in this book is distributed on an "As Is" basis, without warranty. Although every precaution has been taken in the preparation of this body of work to provide accurate information, neither the author nor Anthurium Publishing LLC shall have any liability to any person or entity with respect to any loss or damage caused or alleged to be caused directly or indirectly by the use of the information, suggestions or instructions contained herein or by the use of any devices or software applications described herein. The publisher and the author make no representations or warranties with respect to the accuracy or completeness of the contents and the reader accepts information on the condition that errors or omissions shall not be made the basis for any claim, demand or cause for action. The advice contained herein may not be suitable for every situation and therefore the author and publisher make no claims or warranties that past results will be indicative of future results. If professional assistance is required, the services of a competent professional person should be sought.

Anthurium Publishing LLC provides the synthesis for writers to translate their creative ideas into professionally-published works; converting truth, fiction, poetic thoughts and expertise into a recorded legacy to be read, savored and shared. Every book published by Anthurium Publishing LLC is printed and manufactured in the United States of America.

DEDICATION

To my friend, Ernesta Wright, founder and Executive Director of The G.R.E.E.N. Foundation in Orange County, CA. You are a respected nonprofit colleague and one of the most disciplined grantwriters I know. I continue to be inspired by your vision and persistence as a community champion. You always seem to make great things happen on behalf of others. It has been very exciting to watch you bring your vision to life person-by-person, program-by-program, dollar-by-dollar and grant-by-grant. Your entrepreneurial tenacity and networking talents continue to create new avenues of opportunity and value for everyone fortunate enough to collaborate with you.

"Your book is a fantastic guide to grant writing, very thorough with lots of tremendous writing samples, checklists and other information."

Marshall Howard (1945-2013)
Attorney, television executive and CEO of Marshall Howard & Associates

World's leading business relationship expert and author of "Let's Have Lunch Together"

"The worksheets in this book ask vital questions you must answer in order to develop a competitive grant."

Edward Grice, Associate Dean,
Graduate School of Nonprofit Management, American Jewish University

"The system makes the grant writing process easy to understand and manage."

Karen Blakeney-Granado, M.S., Nonprofit professional and former Executive Director of Chinatown Service Center, Los Angeles, CA

Acknowledgements

To my cousin, Charron Jones, for your meticulous scrutiny of the initial,100-page version of this workbook that I used to teach my workshops for many years. To former employers and supervisors for giving me the opportunity to gain the experience that is now recorded in these pages, especially Ginny Foat, Lorri L. Jean, Darrel Cummings, Kay Ostberg, Pan Fuchs and Tom Miller,

To jazz vocalist Phyllis Battle for your generosity to allow me to host my very first grant writing workshops at your performance workspace, Ja-Phyl's Place in the Leimert Park area of Los Angeles during the late 1990's,

To Cora Alley, my first college English professor who packaged the fundamentals of writing into a "user-friendly" system to lay the groundwork that has shaped my writing ability and style throughout my professional career. To two of the most masterful grantwriters I've ever had the honor of working with and learning from over the years, Craig Vincent-Jones, Executive Director, Commission on HIV at County of Los Angeles and Audrey Thompson, M.A. of Thompson Community Enterprises.

I also extend a special thank you to the following individuals for their generous investment of time in the midst of very busy schedules to review and provide feedback on drafts of the worksheets and portions of this workbook: Edward Grice, M.B.A., Assistant Dean of the Graduate Nonprofit Program, American Jewish University, Bel Air, CA; Lisa Wilson, Director of Organizational Learning and Evaluation, The Flintridge Center, Pasadena, CA; Del Smulowitz and the late Howard Marshall of Marshall Howard & Associates, Bell Canyon, CA; Dr. Lee Draper, President of Draper Consulting Group, Santa Monica, CA; and Annekah Merrielle Hall-Solomon, M.B.A., Assistant Director of Admissions, Claremont Graduate University.

To a partial list of former clients, including Jewel Thais-Williams of Village Healthcare Foundation, Los Angeles, CA who helped me understand the immediate and significant long-term benefits of a plant-based diet and regular exercise; Robin McCarthy, Executive Director, Fire Family Foundation, Los Angeles, CA. Our collaboration when she was Executive Director of Women At Work in Pasadena, CA provided the opportunity for me to fine-tune The Grantbuilder™ system through a series of workshops I conducted there for several years; and finally two longtime friends and colleagues, Karen Blakeney-Granado, M.A. who I had the honor of working with initially at First 5 LA, then later as a grant writing consultant when she served as Executive Director of Chinatown Service Center, Los Angeles, CA, and finally to my walking buddy Laurie Pieper, Director of Finance and Operations at Helpline Youth Counseling, Los Angeles. She hired me as a consultant many years ago when she served as CFO for LAMP, a nonprofit located in the Skidrow area of downtown Los Angeles to serve homeless individuals.

Finally and most importantly, to my family who made sure I had mastered my ABC's and other building blocks for learning before I entered the Federal Head Start program in the 1960's (especially to my aunts, "Bobbi Jean," Carolyn, Christine, Louise and "Sue").
To my mother, Katie and my late father, Alfred Simms for the set of World Book Encyclopedias and home library that introduced me to the vast world of people, places and things that have inspired my inquisitiveness and love of the written word since grade school. To my better half, Adrianne M. Hall, who spent countless hours over the years helping me to copy and assemble hundreds of three-ring binders with the early versions of this workbook. Thank you for being my biggest cheerleader in this effort.

A Personal Introduction from the Author

Grant writing was not even on my radar screen until my boss walked into my office one Thursday afternoon during the mid-1990's. He informed me that he was leaving to go on a business trip the next day and didn't have time to meet the deadline for two grant proposals. For whatever reason, I was the one chosen to complete and submit the two applications by the following Tuesday.

Although I had worked with other staff to compile information for the agency's grant writing consultant on numerous occasions, I had never prepared one by myself. About two months later, when my boss informed me that one of the proposals had been funded for the full $50,000 requested, I knew that I had found my niche – I joined the ranks of grantwriters who have learned the craft through the "other duties as assigned" process, which is typical in the nonprofit sector.

Over the years, I have worked for several nonprofit organizations that cranked grant proposals out like well-oiled machines. This type of "hands on" training has been invaluable. In my roles as a nonprofit administrator for well-established organizations with multi-million dollar budgets, I received numerous invitations to serve on grant review panels. In 2000 I founded a nonprofit arts agency and applied my grant writing skills to securing grants and sponsorships. The agency received funding from state, county, foundation and corporate sources to produce the Instrumental Women® Lady Jazz™ Concert Series in Southern California for nine consecutive years.

Years of designing and managing grant-funded programs have included responsibilities for compliance with funding contracts and grant agreements. This workbook has evolved from an initial set of handouts for grant writing workshops I first offered in Los Angeles during the late 1990's. As the number of handouts began to grow, it became clear that a full-length book was the next logical step.

Professional experience as a nonprofit administrator for more than twenty years has provided me with numerous opportunities to identify funders and develop grant proposals. This includes program design and grant writing for newly-formed grassroots, to large organizations and government agencies with multi-million dollar budgets. As an instructor in the Nonprofit Management and Fundraising Program at UCLA Extension, my knowledge base and skills in grant writing are constantly evolving as I encounter students with new questions, creative approaches and new ideas. The lessons, examples and "hands on" learning activities in The Grantbuilder™ series capture the full range of my experience in this discipline. The 2nd Edition includes updated information on online and e-applications.

People often ask grantwriters, "Is money available?" The answer is a resounding, "Yes." Standards and expectations of funders and applicants continue to evolve in response to constant changes in community needs, economic conditions and technology. Today's "best practices" often become tomorrow's outdated, ineffective methods. However, one of the keys to success in securing grant money is the mastery of a basic "how to" list, including: Designing your program, locating the most appropriate funding sources, and finally, preparing and submitting the most competitive grant proposals possible. This workbook is divided into nine sections, with each designed to equip you with the full set of knowledge, tools and skills to master the fundamentals needed for grant writing success.

The Grantbuilder™ Step-by-Step Guide To Grant Writing Workbook

Contents

Part VI: Budget Development & Timeline   125

Part VII: Workplan (Timeline, Scope of Work)   151

The Grantbuilder™
Step-by-Step Grant Writing Process

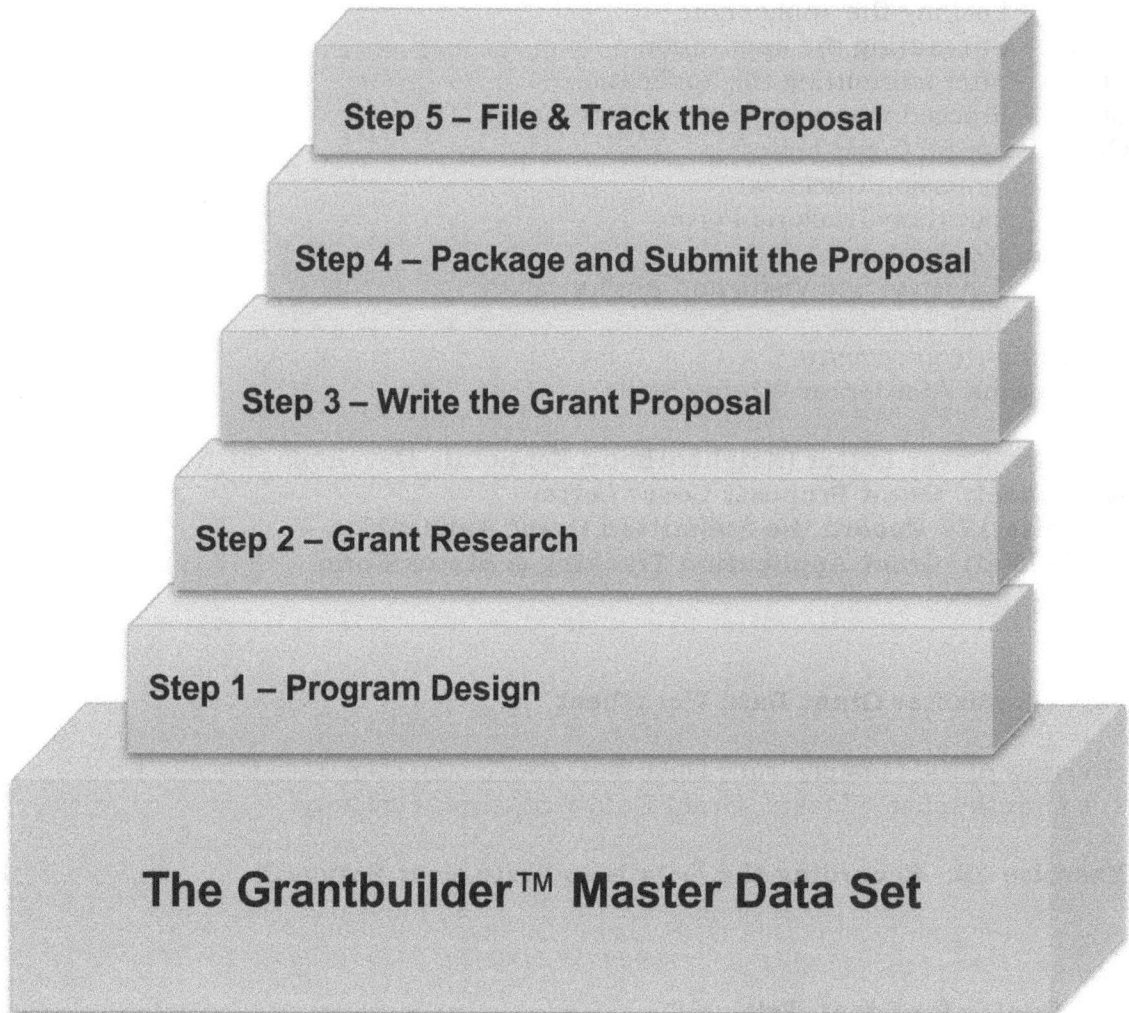

Step 5 – File & Track the Proposal

Step 4 – Package and Submit the Proposal

Step 3 – Write the Grant Proposal

Step 2 – Grant Research

Step 1 – Program Design

The Grantbuilder™ Master Data Set

This table is included to make it easier to locate each of the tables, illustrations, worksheets and learning exercises as you proceed through the workbook.

Page(s)	Table #	Illustration #	Worksheet	Exercise #	The Grant Builder™ Directory of Learning Tools Name/Description
3	1				Common Grant Categories
4	2				Funding Sources
8		1			The Grant Application Process
10	3				LOI's, LOA's and LOR's
13	4				Program Duration and Funding Sources
14		2			Government Funding Streams
19	5				Sampling of Funding Sources and Categories
20				1	Identify Potential Government Funding Sources
22	6				IRS Subsection Codes for Tax-Exempt Organizations
32	7				Four Common Types of Nonprofit Collaborative Agreements
35			✓		Memorandum of Understanding (MOU)
37				2	Identify Potential Collaborators
44				3	Locating Grants on the Internet: Corporate Giving
45	8				Federal Agencies with Grant Making Programs
48				4	Locating Grants on the Internet: Government Grants
55	9				Purpose for the Letter of Interest or Letter of Application
74		3			The 10 Most Common Grant Proposal Information Categories
76-77			✓		Grant Application Review Worksheet
83			✓		Grant Proposal Development Worksheet
78				5	Reviewing Grant Applications
87				6	Preparing the Grant Proposal Development Worksheet (aka "Application Checklist" and "Grant Proposal Development Outline")
94				7	Developing Your Program Design
95-97			✓		Program Design Worksheet
101				8	Identifying Basic Sections in Grant Proposals
114	10				Formatting Guidelines
117		4			Laying the Groundwork for E-apps
121				9	Create Your Grant Application Template
121				10	Develop an Initial Draft of the Proposal Narrative
122				11	Preparing the Final Draft
123				12	Preparing for Formatting Requirements
132	11				Full-time Equivalents (FTE's)
133			✓		Wage & Salary Calculations Worksheet
137				13	Developing the Budget
138-143					Budget Worksheet
144				14	Preparing the Budget Justification
146			✓		Budget Justification Worksheet
148				15	Preparing the Budget Narrative
149			✓		Budget Narrative Worksheet
156				16	Preparing the Workplan
168			✓		Grant Proposal Cover Letter Worksheet
170				17	Record Submitted Grant Applications
171			✓		Grant Application Tracking & Status Form
184-231			✓		Master Grant Data Worksheet (directory of contents on pages 182-183)

For updates and additional grant writing resources

visit www.TheGrantbuilder.com

Introduction to Grant Writing and The Grantbuilder™ System

Grant writing is the practice of preparing applications and proposals to request support from funding sources that provide cash grants. Sources include government, corporations, foundations, trusts and in limited instances, wealthy individuals. The professionals who perform this task don't actually "write grants," rather they prepare documents in specific formats to "request" grants. The process is known as grant writing and those who perform the task are referred to as grantwriters.

> Technically and historically, the terms **grant writing** and **grant writer** have been presented as separate words. In recent decades, particularly in current nonprofit and business publications, the use of these terms as compound nouns is common.

Grantwriters are by hired by educational institutions, government agencies, faith-based organizations and nonprofit organizations. Some work as full-time or part-time staff and some freelance as independent consultants.

Most people seek training in grant writing for one of the following reasons:
1) The need to find funds for an existing charitable organization or program,
2) The need to find funds for a new idea or project that will benefit the community,
3) Interest in pursuing a career as a grant writer in a full-time or part-time staff position, or
4) To work as an independent consultant, or as a full-time career or to create supplemental income.

Successful grant writing entails the mastery of fundamentals and the application of certain skills, all which are introduced in this workbook. This workbook walks you through the entire process required to plan, write and submit grant proposals that adhere to professional grantmaking standards. This training system introduces the grant writing process through a sequence of building blocks, "lessons," that include examples, sample grant application documents and "hands on" learning activities.

This workbook is designed with a step-by-step sequence of lessons and exercises that culminate with an activity to complete an actual grant application. Two sample proposals, complete with budgets, are included in The Grantbuilder™ Workbook. One is a brief Letter of Interest (LOI) and the other is a full proposal.

The Grantbuilder™ set of proprietary worksheets provide opportunities for new and experienced grantwriters to apply newly-learned knowledge to prepare actual grant applications and proposals. All worksheets introduced in The Grantbuilder™ Workbook are available in both hardcopy and digital versions. Visit www.TheGrantbuilder.com for information on pricing and ordering, including a discount available with the purchase of each 2nd Edition of this workbook.

The Grantbuilder™ is a professional education program for new and experienced grantwriters. Those new to the profession will receive an introduction and learning activities to master the fundamentals. Experienced grantwriters will recognize the time-saving aspects of consolidating all of the information needed to prepare grants for an organization into the proprietary **Master Grant Data Worksheet**.

The design for The Grantbuilder™ System is influenced by elements and processes used in the construction industry. Specifically, the analogy of designing, planning, constructing and maintaining a house can serve as the frame of reference for learning how to build grant applications.

This system teaches grant writing as a step-by-step process, starting with an introduction to the basics to lay a strong foundation. Every industry has its own language, guidelines and nuances. This system integrates all of those factors, starting with an overview of grantmaking. Who give grants? Who can apply? How to apply? What information is needed to apply? This workbook answers these and other questions relevant to locating funding sources, preparing grant applications and securing grant awards.

Approximately 90% of information required on grant applications is similar from funder to funder, however, the format and sequence of information may be different. If you were to tour five different homes that have four bedrooms and two baths, each would be unique in color scheme, furnishings and how it is decorated. Take another example of kitchens in two different homes. Both have most of the same components (i.e. stove, refrigerator, microwave, sink), but one may have a trash compactor and dishwasher, and certainly each will have its own floor plan and personal touches.

These examples illustrate the similarities and differences among funders and grant applications. Structural elements and major systems like the foundation, electrical, plumbing and roof can be compared to the major categories of information found in all grant applications. The choice of colors and the selection and placement of furnishings are used to distinguish the individual preferences and style of each homeowner. Likewise, each grant application must be tailored to the specific preferences of the funding source as it relates to content and format.

This Grantbuilder™ System provides a step-by-step overview of the fundamentals. Our proprietary series of easy-to-use worksheets provides a "hands-on" learning exercise for each topic covered in the grant writing process. Each activity is a building block, designed to equip the grantwriter with an expanded base of knowledge, skills and tools proven effective in securing grant funds.

One of the primary distinctions of this system is the **Grantbuilder™ Master Grant Data Worksheet**. This multi-page tool makes it easy to capture, record, organize and retrieve every category of information needed for all types of funders and applications. It can be used to consolidate information that may currently exist in multiple documents and filing systems. Once completed, this document can serve as a centralized database, a master template that contains all of the information needed to prepare all types of grant applications for any organization.

We trust you will find the Grantbuilder™ system useful to streamline the grant writing process. This approach equips you to prepare more grants in less time, resulting in increased opportunities for funding on an ongoing basis.

NOTES

Part I: Introduction to Grants

This section provides an overview of grants, including major sources of government, corporate and foundation funding. It also discusses the categories of organizations eligible to apply for grants, as well as the role of collaborations.

Upon the completion of Part I, you will be able to:

- Describe the major categories of funding sources

- Identify funding sources and access grant application guidelines

- Understand the importance of a 501(c)(3) organization as it relates to soliciting and securing grants

- Establish collaborative agreements with existing 501(c)(3)'s and other community organizations

As you proceed with the completion of exercises in this workbook, concurrently it is important to begin the process of collecting and recording information onto the **Master Grant Data Worksheet** (Pages 180-231). If you will follow this recommendation, you will have all of the information needed to prepare any type of grant application by the time you complete this workbook.

What is a grant?

A grant is a certain amount of money "granted" or given to an individual or organization for a specific purpose. A grant is not a loan and does <u>not</u> have to be repaid. However, there are always certain conditions, rules or restrictions that accompany any grant award.

Grantmaking is a term associated with all of the activities involved in the process to request and award funds in the form of grants. The act of grantmaking is one form of charitable giving. Think of a grant as a type of structured donation. Money is awarded in response to a written request made in the form of a grant application or proposal. The request is prepared according to guidelines established by the funding source, or by following basic guidelines used in the grantmaking profession.

All funders engaged in grantmaking have some type of standard application process in place. They also have a set of expectations that accompany their grant awards, which are expressed in a written grant agreement.

Most grants are awarded for a one-year time period. The time period is also referred to as the *grant cycle* or *funding cycle*. Some funders offer grants for multi-year time periods. The most common categories of grants are described in Table 1 on the following page.

A *grantor* "awards" grant funds to a *grantee*.

Common Grant Categories

Table 1

Funding Category	Brief Description	Example(s)
Program Grants *Also referred to as* **designated** *or* **restricted** *grants, the funds must be used only for the purpose for which the grant was awarded.*	Awarded to support a specific program or project as described in the applicant's funding proposal, and as stipulated in the grant agreement	After-school tutoring program, summer recreation program for seniors, field trips for special needs adults
General Operating Grants	Awarded to support the agency overall	Funds may be used for anything that the agency needs to operate in accordance with its primary mission and purpose
Special Initiatives	Created when a foundation makes the decision to devote all or some of its funding to address a limited number of issues	Reducing childhood obesity; food pantry and nutritional services for families in an area recently impacted by a natural disaster; encouraging nonprofits to become more energy efficient; etc.
Capital	Awarded to support the renovation, purchase and/or construction of facilities, as well as major infrastructure investments like computer systems	Fees to an architect to design a new day care center; repaving a parking lot
Challenge ("Matching")	Awarded as an incentive for the recipient to "raise" or "match" funds from some other funding source for a specific project	A $150,000 grant awarded with a 1:1 requirement that an additional $150,000 in matching funds is secured from other sources within a specific time period

Funding Sources

There are a variety of resources available to research and prepare proposals. Based on the type of community project or service of interest to you, there is definitely some type of funding source available. Grants provide support for programs that address health, education, arts, social services, environmental, faith-based and other areas that provide benefit to some segment of the public.

The question is, "What do you need to do to get the funds?" Learning and mastering the fundamental building blocks for grant writing success is the starting point. Becoming familiar with the types of grants available, including how and where to find them are among the first steps. This process is referred to as grants research.

There are literally thousands of funding sources for almost any "worthy cause." The three main sources for grants are: government, corporate and foundation. This is good news for those in search of grant funds to implement, maintain or expand community programs. The following table presents the three major categories of funders and their primary reasons for grantmaking, with additional information provided on the following page.

Funding Sources

Table 2

Main Categories	Goals & Objectives
Government • Federal • State • Regional (county, district, etc.) • Local (city)	To support legislation by providing funding to implement, maintain and expand activities that have received budget approval by the governing body. *Example: State grant given to a city to renovate a library*
Foundations • Publicly-funded • Corporate • Private • Family • Community	To support specific types of "worthy causes" as determined by the directors or managers of the foundation. *Example: Foundation gives grant to local school for a community garden on campus*
Corporations (for-profit)	To attract additional customers over the long-term and increase sales To support "worthy causes" To gain greater corporate visibility

Funders usually provide specific information about the types of programs and activities that they will or will not support. Some funding guidelines include a "Do Not Fund" list with specific categories of activities that will not be considered.

Government Grant Sources

The categories and dollar amounts of grants available from government entities are dictated by legislation. Laws and regulations may be initiated by events that attract widespread public attention, or in response to an unexpected catastrophe. There are numerous grant opportunities at all levels of government, as referenced below:

Federal grants are awarded by branches or divisions of the federal government. (Example: U.S. Department of Education, U.S. Department of Homeland Security, etc.)

State grants are awarded by a branch or division of state government. (Example: Department of Health, Social Services Department, etc.)

Regional/County grants are awarded by a branch or division of the regional/county government. (Example: County Arts Commission, Tri-State Office of Family Health, etc.)

Local/City grants are awarded by a branch or division of the local/city government. (Example: Housing Department, Public Health Division, etc.)

Public Officials may have decision-making authority for discretionary funds or other resources that have been designated for certain programs and activities. (Example: A State Senator may have a budget to award grants or to sponsor events, a City Councilmember may be able to secure a public facility for an event at a reduced cost or at no cost to nonprofit organizations.)

Foundation Grants

Also called "charitable foundations," grantmaking foundations are established for the purpose of providing donations and support to other organizations, or to provide funding support for specific charitable purposes determined by the foundation. An example is a sportswear manufacturer that establishes a foundation to fund athletic activities.

There are two categories of foundations, public and private. The category is often an indication of how they derive their funds, mainly from public or private sources. The governing board of a foundation determines the parameters for its grantmaking priorities and decisions. The number of staff employed by a foundation, has no correlation to the amount of grant funds they have available.

Corporate Foundation Grants are awarded by **private foundations** that have been established by incorporated, for-profit businesses. This type of private foundation derives the majority of its income from the profits of the corporation. (Example: Starbucks Foundation, Walmart Foundation, etc.)

Some corporations provide cash sponsorships in addition to or in lieu of grants. Sometimes sponsorships are processed through the same department as grants, however the application process usually differs.

5

Private Foundation Grants are awarded by a foundation that has typically been established by an individual or family. (Example: Bill & Melinda Gates Foundation, Magic Johnson Foundation, etc.) The IRS requires that private foundations meet or exceed paying out a minimum of 5% each year of their net assets for charitable purposes, including qualifying distributions.

> *A private foundation must pay out at least 5% of the value of its holdings each year. This is most often the source of funds for their grant awards.*

Family Foundation Grants are awarded by a nonprofit that has been established with funds from members of a single family. A family foundation is a type of private foundation. At least one family member maintains involvement as a donor, is required to serve as an officer or board member, and plays a major role in managing the foundation. (Example: Tiger Woods Foundation, Doug Flute Jr. Foundation for Autism, etc.)

Community Foundation Grants are awarded by nonprofits that have been established as vehicles to pool donations from a variety of sources for the purpose of facilitating the investment into charitable causes within a specific geographic region. (Example: Community Foundation of Central Missouri, California Community Foundation, etc.)

Additional Grant Classifications

Matching grants may be awarded by government, corporate or foundation sources and require that the recipient "raise" or "match" funds at a certain amount from some other funding source for the proposed project.

Example A: A one-to-one (1:1) match means that each dollar of grant funds must be matched with one dollar raised from some other source.

Grant Award	$ 30,000
Required Match	30,000
Total Program	$ 60,000

Example B: A three-to-one (3:1) match means that for every three dollars of grant funds received, one dollar must be raised from some other source.

Grant Award	$ 30,000
Required Match	10,000
Total Program	$ 40,000

Challenge grants are a type of **matching** grant. Some funders provide them as incentives to encourage grantees to raise the matching portion needed to fund a specific application request. A challenge grant may also be used as leverage to attract other funders and donors to give, and to reduce future dependency on the funder. This type of grant usually requires a match of "cash" or "inkind" resources. Inkind resources are goods or services donated to your project. See page 134 for more information on "inkind" donations.

Challenge grants are a wonderful fundraising incentive. Look for signs that a funder is open to structuring their grant as a challenge grant, and whenever appropriate, suggest to a funder that you would like to use their grant as a challenge grant to leverage additional funding from other sources.

Renewable grants may be awarded for a specified number of funding cycles, contingent upon the grantee's performance. Typically, each cycle is a 12-month period, which may be eligible for "renewal" for one or more years. Renewal is always based on whether or not the program met the objectives presented in the original proposal and operated in compliance with the grant agreement.

> Example C: A 3-year renewable grant totaling $150,000 indicates that the funding will be awarded for a total of $50,000* each year, assuming that the recipient complies with the conditions of the grant agreement during each funding cycle. *Based on an equal amount each year calculated as follows: $150,000 ÷ 3 years.

> *Renewable and Non-Competitive Grants*
> *This type of grant is basically "guaranteed" for the duration of a multi-year funding period as long as the grantee performs according to the grant agreement (assuming the grantor has funds available in subsequent years)*

Non-Competitive grants usually coincide with **renewable** grants. After the first funding cycle for a renewable grant, the recipient does not have to "compete" with other new or existing applicants in order to have the funding renewed.

> Example: If a recipient has performed well during the first year of a three-year grant, funding is typically awarded automatically during the following year as long as the recipient is operating the program in accordance with the initial agreement.

Competitive grants indicate that the applicant will be "competing" with other applicants for the same source of funds.

The Grant Application Process

All funders have developed their own processes to announce, receive and review applications to make decisions about grant awards. There are certain categories of information required by all funders, whether they require the submission of a traditional hardcopy application or an online application. The Grantbuilder™ Training System provides you with the tools to complete applications for all types of grants.

The terms *grant application* and *grant proposal (or "proposal")* are used interchangeably. The term *application* sometimes refers to the standard form(s) that have to be filled-in and submitted along with the narrative section of the proposal and any other attachments required by the funder.

> **The term "grant application" is used interchangeably with the term "grant proposal"**

Each application should be prepared according to guidelines provided by the perspective funder. Once an appropriate funding source has been identified, the grantwriter must complete a certain sequence of steps to complete the application.

The Grantbuilder™ System employs a sequence of major steps, which are illustrated below and described on the following page. Each major step requires the completion of specific activities to proceed to the next phase in building a grant application. The large arrow represents the Master Grant Data Worksheet that begins on page 180. The multi-page worksheet is designed to make it easy to capture all categories of information for any agency or program. Once completed, information can be edited and updated on an ongoing basis.

Illustration 1

The Grant Application Process

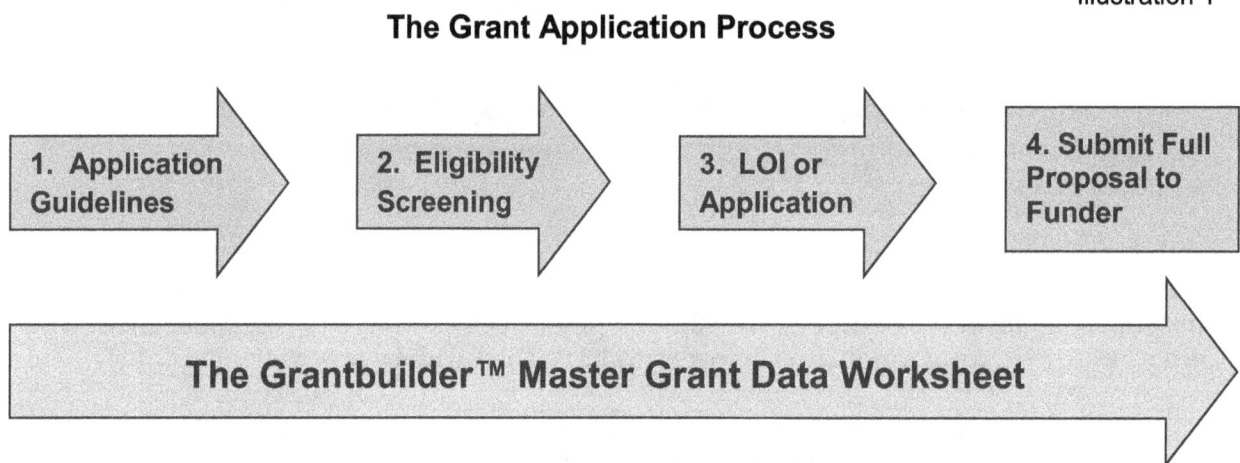

1. Application Guidelines → 2. Eligibility Screening → 3. LOI or Application → 4. Submit Full Proposal to Funder

The Grantbuilder™ Master Grant Data Worksheet

You should review the entire worksheet as soon as possible, so that you can become familiar with all categories of information you will need to gather about your programs to complete the worksheet as you proceed through the remainder of this workbook. This way, you will have all of the information organized in a centralized system, which will provide you with everything needed to create a master grant template. You will be able to use and update this document to prepare grant applications for an organization on an ongoing basis.

The Grant Application Process

1. Application Guidelines

The potential applicant reviews information about the funding opportunity, which may provide additional instructions to obtain a standard application form or other guidelines.

2. Eligibility Screening

Most funders provide a list of requirements that a potential applicant must meet. Some use an "eligibility quiz" that makes it easy for the potential applicant to determine if they qualify to apply. This will inform whether it is appropriate and worthwhile to invest additional time to go through the process of completing and submitting an application.

For applications that are prepared and submitted using a funder's e-application system, a potential applicant typically starts the process by answering a series of eligibility questions at the funder's website. If the responses indicate that all eligibility requirements are met, the applicant will receive online instructions or prompts to proceed to the full application. If applicable, a password will be provided to access the application. The system will also provide instructions regarding how to navigate through the application to complete it.

3. LOI or Application

Some funders accept and review grant proposals from all applicants who meet their eligibility requirements. Others require an initial Letter of Inquiry, known as an "LOI" (see description on the following page). Think of the LOI as an introduction to provide the funder with a quick overview of the grant request. After reviewing the LOI, the funder may make a request for the applicant to submit a full proposal.

4. Deliver to Funder

The completed application is submitted to the funder, who will then complete a formal review process to determine if the applicant will be awarded a grant.

The Grantbuilder™ Master Grant Data Worksheet

LOI's and LOA's

Some funding sources require a *"Letter of Intent"* or *"Letter of Inquiry" (LOI)* as a first step. An LOI provides a brief overview of your organization and program for initial screening purposes. For hard copy formats, an LOI is usually two to three pages maximum. Funders review LOI's to determine whether the request is aligned with their current funding goals and whether the proposed grant is of interest to them. If it is, and they have funds available, they may extend an invitation for the applicant to submit a full proposal. Samples and instructions for preparing LOI's are included on pages 52 – 60.

For government funders, an LOI serves a different purpose. It is also used to help the funder determine the total number of potential applicants, the projected total of anticipated grant requests, the types of programs or services proposed, and the geographic regions and target populations that will be represented or served by the proposed grants. Variations of this document are presented in the following table.

LOI's, LOA's and LOR's

Table 3

Type of Document	Description of Primary Use
Letter of Intent (LOI)	"Letter of Intent to Apply for Funding" - Required by some government funders to determine the potential number of applications to expect in response to an announcement that grants are available. This type of LOI is commonly a prerequisite for submitting an application to a government funding source.
Letter of Inquiry* (LOI)	May refer to a literal "inquiry" to a funder to get information on current or future funding opportunities. Unless a funder specifically states they do not accept unsolicited inquires, an agency may prepare this type of LOI to introduce itself to a funder.
Letter of Interest* (LOI)	Conveys "interest" in being included on a funder's list to be invited to submit a proposal; It may also serve to introduce an organization to a funder.
Letter of Introduction (LOI)	Used by the nonprofit to "introduce" itself to a funding source.
Letter of Application (LOI)	When a funder requests an LOA, it usually serves as the grant application. It is sometimes referred to as a "mini-proposal."
Letter of Request (LOR)	Usually the same as a Letter of Application. Not as common as LOI's and LOA's

*These terms sometimes refer to the same type of document.

The funder will provide instructions if a specific format and content are required for an LOI, LOA or LOR. For non-government funders, a *Letter of Intent* may also serve as a screening tool to be sure that the proposed program fits within their scope of funding interests. This document typically includes basic information on the applicant organization, programs and services offered, target population served and an indication of what will be proposed for funding. A *Letter of Inquiry* is sometimes used interchangeably with the *Letter of Interest.* It should be a very brief (one-page) letter to a potential funder to introduce an applicant organization and to request information on their guidelines and application process. See pages 54-56 for more information on LOI's and LOA's specific to corporate and foundation funders.

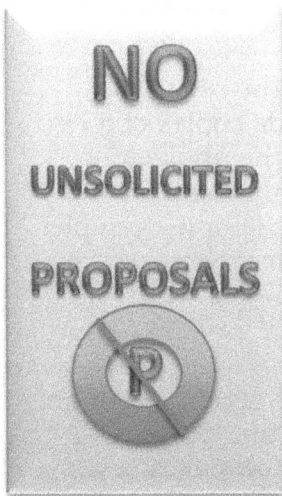

A *closed application* ("by invitation only") process exists when the funder does not accept unsolicited proposals and will consider applications only from programs they have pre-selected. In effect, only potential grantees who have been "invited" to submit grant proposals are considered. In some instances, this type of funder may accept a *Letter of Introduction* or *Letter of Inquiry from* a potential applicant as a first step.

An *open application* process exists when the funder will accept proposals from any eligible organization or program. Applicants may also be required to meet additional criteria (i.e. must be a licensed clinic to apply for a health services grant; must hire a credentialed educator to head a literacy program). An open application process may also refer to grants that have no application deadlines, with applications accepted on an ongoing basis.

Government Grants

Funds for government grants come from the public coffers, generated by taxes collected from individuals and businesses. Government grants have very detailed application instructions, including the types of programs and activities that can be funded. These are typically the most detailed and time consuming applications to prepare due to the related background information that needs to be reviewed regarding the funding opportunity. This may include a number of standard forms and other technical or statistical data that must be submitted as part of the application. One example is a *board resolution*, which is a document indicating that the executive director (or other agency representative) has received authorization from the agency's board of directors to apply for the grant.

Much of the extra paperwork associated with government grants is the result of legislation that applies to some aspect of the grant. This may include copies of a nonprofit's written policies and procedures, or forms included with the application that must be signed and submitted to acknowledge that the applicant has read, understood and agrees to comply with certain rules, guidelines, etc. (Some examples of forms include: Drug Free Workplace Policy, Living Wage Ordinance, Non-Discrimination Policy, Conflict of Interest Disclosure, etc.)

Since all government grants are the result of some type of legislative action, there are numerous rules and regulations incorporated into the grant application process. A completed application for a government grant may be as short as a few pages or as long as several hundred pages.

How do government grant funds originate?

Political and social issues serve as the impetus for all sources of government funding. It is often the result of politicians introducing legislation to address a specific societal or business issue. Once approved, new funding may be authorized to support the new legislation. In some instances, a certain amount or a percent of funds is budgeted and approved for distribution as grants. Some of the funds may be reserved to provide grants to other government applicants. However, a portion may be allocated to categories in which schools, hospitals and other community-based organizations are eligible to apply.

State or local jurisdictions may impose a special tax to fund certain types of programs or services. In other instances, they may identify an existing fund to use for this purpose. The larger the city or jurisdiction, or the greater their respective budget for discretionary funds, the greater the likelihood that some categories of grants may be available. (Examples: A tax on boating licenses to provide grants for water-related recreational activities for local organizations; a surcharge on hotel rooms to provide grants for free public festivals to encourage tourism)

Sources of Government Grants

All government grants are funded by some combination of tax dollars or similar levies. Funds that originate at the federal level can provide grants directly to states, county or regional jurisdictions, cities or local municipalities, directly to community-based organizations, and in very limited instances, to individuals.

There are a variety of grants available, from multi-million dollar grants awarded to major universities for research and development (R&D), to grants of several thousand dollars awarded to small, after-school athletic programs. *Table 8 on page 45 includes a list of the 26 federal agencies that operate grantmaking programs as of 2014.*

Laws that govern the grantmaking process for federal agencies have a far-reaching impact on laws and guidelines for how grants are awarded by all categories of funders in the U.S. that provide grants. Becoming knowledgeable of the standards and guidelines associated with federal grants will lay a solid foundation for understanding fundamentals that apply to all grants.

Some government departments have a long history of grantmaking, supporting programs on an ongoing basis or issuing grants for special initiatives. The following table highlights a few examples of sources and purposes for funding of various durations.

Program Duration and Funding Sources

Table 4

Program Duration	Description of Funding Source or Funding Purpose
Ongoing	Examples of funding sources: • Department of Education • Department of Transportation • Health & Human Resources Administration
Special Initiatives *Usually time-limited, but may be long-term*	Examples of funding objectives: • Program to manage an anticipated or prolonged drought that has an adverse impact on a region's water resources • Program to improve air quality • Program to support construction in an area that needs to be rebuilt due to a natural disaster (i.e. hurricane, earthquake, wild fires)

Pages 15 through 19 provide an overview of all major categories of grant funding sources, including a detailed description of the entire grantmaking process used to award federal grants. A section is also devoted to corporate and foundation grants.

Government Funding Streams

Funding streams describe the various routes or "streams" that government money travels through from grantors to grantees. Becoming knowledgeable about funding streams can be very advantageous to grantwriters and applicant organizations. Knowing where the money originates and the route it takes will equip you with knowledge to be proactive in identifying and approaching more potential funding sources. The following diagram illustrates the various routes that government grant funds can take.

Illustration 2

Government Funding Streams

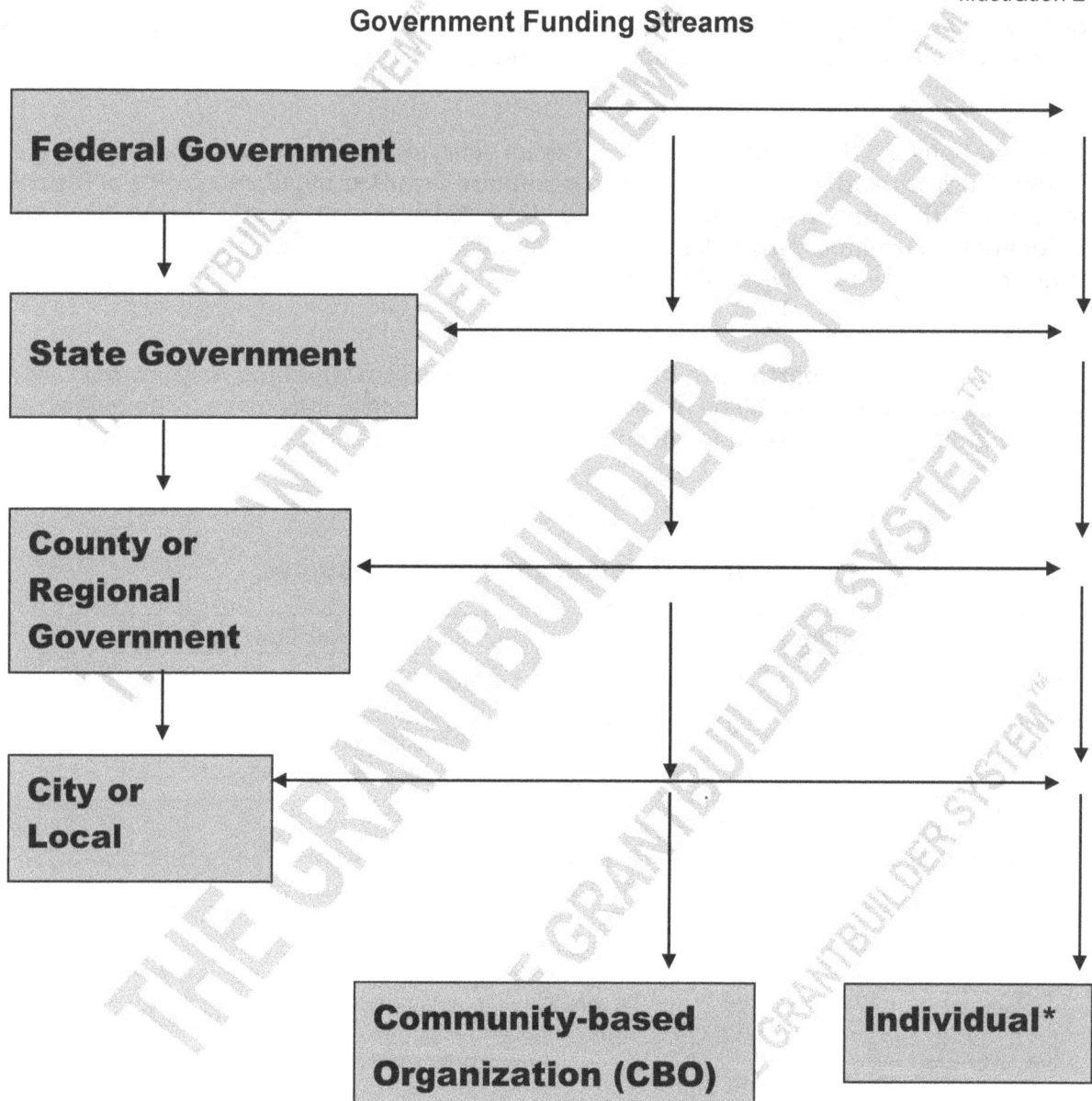

*Government grants to individuals for community programs and services are very rare. They are most common in the arts and are usually awarded to individual curators to create or complete a specific project, or for consultants providing specialized services to a public or private nonprofit arts organization.

An Overview of the Federal Grant Making Process

Applicants typically become aware of government funding opportunities upon learning of "funding announcements" which are commonly associated with a number of acronyms like RFA's, FOA's, etc. The names used to identify grant applications vary by federal agency. Some of the most common are Requests for Applications (RFA's), Request for Proposals (RFP's), Funding Opportunity Announcement (FOA) and Notice of Funding Availability (NOFA). Federal agencies issue announcements to notify potential applicants of upcoming funding opportunities. This process provides potential applicants with information to determine if they are eligible and if it is feasible to apply. A unique I.D. number is assigned to each government application to distinguish it from other grant opportunities.

The funding announcement will provide information on how to obtain application information. Applications provide the details needed by potential applicants and are usually posted on the funder's website and may be distributed via e-mail. This is the most cost effective and efficient way for potential applicants to review and download information. In addition, many funders post announcements on bulletin boards in their offices that are accessible to the public. Some provide this information to potential applicants via regular mail, but this practice has diminished due to the cost benefits of using the internet and other modes of digital communication.

Most government departments hold one or more *Bidders' Conferences* (also referred to as grant information meetings) prior to the application deadline. This meeting may be conducted in person, online (i.e. webinar) or via teleconference. *Additional information on these sessions is provided on the following page.*

Government grant applications usually include scoring criteria so that applicants will know how much weight is assigned to each question or item that requires a response. It is common to see a total possible score or weight of 100% for an application. Applicants are required to earn a minimum score to be considered for funding. The

government funding agency will initiate a review process of all of the applications received to make a decision about grant awards.

Note: Request for Quotes **(RFQ's)** is a type of funding announcement primarily used by government departments and large corporations. RFQ's are issued to solicit "bids" from potential vendors (individuals, businesses and organizations) to provide goods or services through a vendor contract agreement. They may also be referred to as Request for Bids **(RFB's).** Not typically affiliated with grants, RFQ's also include eligibility requirements and guidelines for applicants.

Grant Review Panel

A grant review committee is convened by the funding source to review and assign a score to each completed application submitted. This group may consist of a mix of the funder's staff, paid consultants or volunteers. The individuals are selected based on their knowledge, experience and expertise as it relates to the type of project being funded.

Some committees are simply asked to assign scores and rank all of the applications. In this instance, the funder will have a process in place to make final decisions about which applicants will receive grant awards. However, some committees may be entrusted with determining the final slate of grantees, along with recommended grant amounts.

Funding Recommendations

Announce Grant Awards

Each federal department that offers grants has its own process to issue announcements about grant awards. Successful applicants may receive an initial notification by phone, e-mail, regular mail or other means (i.e. announcement at a public meeting). However, the funding source will also be required to make the list of successful grantees and amounts available to the public. This is usually accomplished with a post to the funder's website and may entail an e-blast to notify all applicants of the outcome. Declination notices are sent to the applicants who were not selected for funding.

As illustrated below, the government grant making process can be described using a simple, three-step process, with a specific date applicable to each step.

Step #3: Grant Agreement

Step #2: Formal, Legislative Approval of Grant Award Recommendations

Step #1: Announcement of Grant Award(s)

Bidders' Conferences and Information Sessions

Bidders Conferences are convened to allow potential applicants time to ask any questions relating to the grant application and guidelines. Convened and facilitated by staff from the department offering the grant opportunity, these meetings are always free of charge and may be convened online as a webinar, via phone as a teleconference, in a government office or other public setting.

Attendance at this type of meeting may be one of the eligibility requirements to submit an application. In the event that a funder states, "Attendance/Participation is recommended" but not necessarily required, it is always advisable to participate. They may announce corrections to parts of the application instructions or important updates that weren't included in the original printed application. There may also be unexpected, last minute requirements or adjustments that were not stated in the initial version of the application.

A list of all questions presented during one of these sessions (along with corresponding answers) is usually posted on the funder's website or distributed to all participants via e-mail. The funder may allow additional questions to be submitted up to a specified date, which will always precede the grant application deadline.

Technical Assistance (TA)

Government funders always provide some level of technical assistance (TA) for a grant application. The purpose of TA is to answer questions and provide clarity regarding anything involving the application and the process. TA does not provide any assistance with the "how to's" of the grant writing process, but may provide details, suggestions or insights that can be very helpful in preparing a more competitive proposal.

The timeline for TA always occurs prior to the application deadline. Assistance is usually available up to a certain date before the application deadline. The RFP instructions will indicate if TA is available, along with contact information for the appropriate individual(s) or department. The instructions will stipulate whether the assistance can be accessed via the funder's website, phone, e-mail or other means.

Corporate and Foundation Grants

Corporate and foundation grant applications are typically shorter and easier to prepare than most government grants. Funds are made available through the generosity of profitable enterprises or individuals who have set up foundations or endowments. These grantmakers exist and operate for the purpose of "giving back" to the community at-large, or to focus on one or more specific worthy causes.

Corporate Grants

Many corporations give because they truly believe in giving back to the communities that make it possible for them to generate profits. Some of them adopt the adage, "Doing good is good business." Others use their grantmaking activities to leverage their marketing outreach by supporting groups that represent their primary customer base. "How will you publicize this grant award?" is a question commonly found on applications for grantmaking programs affiliated with for-profit corporations.

Corporate grants come from profits generated by business operations. Although some corporations coordinate all their grant giving through one of their designated departments or divisions, others establish separate foundations for the sole purpose of providing grants. Some prefer to streamline their grantmaking by processing all their related charitable giving through the following types of organizations established specifically for that purpose:

- Nationally-recognized organizations like The United Way

- Community Foundations – there are more than 650 throughout the U.S. Most provide funding within a defined geographic area in proximity to their headquarters. To find potential resources in your area, visit: **www.communityfoundations.net.**

"Giving back" to the community is a win-win for both the corporation and the grantee. The corporation demonstrates support for a program or organization in the community while simultaneously promoting its trade name and services or products. The money that a corporation donates, or grants to charity, is a deductible business expense (i.e. tax write off). Some of which would have otherwise been paid in corporate taxes. Having a structured charitable giving program also provides them with control over what types of causes and organizations their funds support. Corporations with charitable giving programs may give grants to organizations that range from several hundred dollars to six figures. The amount(s) are dependent upon the types and scopes of projects and the amounts the corporation's board of directors allocates for grants.

Advertisement for public events such as community art shows, museum exhibits, walk-a-thons, 10K runs, etc. often features the name(s) of one or more corporate sponsors that have provided grant funds or sponsorship for the event.

Although much of the information needed for grant proposals and corporate sponsorships of community programs and event is very similar, the format and approach is different.

Although the system and tools introduced in this workbook are applicable to all categories of grants, many of our examples are focused on the development of grant proposals to foundations.

Foundation Grants

There are different classifications of foundations, including:

- Corporate foundations – established by and usually funded by an affiliated corporate business entity (e.g. Boeing Foundation, Sony USA Foundation, Starbucks Foundation, Toyota Foundation)

- Publicly-funded foundations and endowments (e.g. L.A. Care Health Plan, National Endowment of the Arts, National Science Foundation)

- Private foundations and endowments (e.g. Mr. Holland's Opus Foundation, Paul Newman Foundation, Susan G. Komen Foundation, Tiger Woods Foundation)

Examples of Various Funding Sources

The following chart provides an example of four different grant sources. Each includes an example of one funding category along with an example of a specific department or entity that issues grants for activities within that category.

Sampling of Funding Sources and Categories

Table 5

Type of Funding	Funding Category	Funding Source
Federal Government	HIV/AIDS services	HRSA (Health Resources & Services Administration) www.hrsa.gov
State Government	Arts (visual & performing)	Texas Commission on the Arts www.arts.state.tx.us
Private Foundation	Community Health	Robert Wood Johnson Foundation www.rwjf.org
Corporate Foundation	After School Program for Youth	Ford Foundation www.fordfoundation.org

Exercise 1 – Identify Potential Government Funding Sources

This learning activity is designed to familiarize you with public funding streams.

Instructions: Using the internet, your local phone directory or other resources, complete the following chart with the name, mailing address and web address of at least one government department/division responsible for overseeing or operating programs in at least three program areas of interest to you. A sampling of 12 program areas is provided below for reference, but you may include any other program areas of interest to you:

Aging	Housing	Economic Development
Arts	Forestry	Social Services
Education	Fire & Safety	Transportation
Health	Seniors	Environment

Name of government entity, dept. or agency	Program Area
1. Local (i.e. city):	
Name of **local** grant program: Contact info: Website:	
2. Regional (i.e. county):	
Name of **local** grant program: Contact info: Website:	
3. State	
Name of **local** grant program: Contact info: Website:	
4. Federal	
Name of **local** grant program: Contact info: Website:	

What is a 501(c)(3)?

The 501(c)(3) is a public benefit corporation. This federal designation indicates the tax-exempt status that has been assigned to an organization by the Internal Revenue Service (IRS). The numbering system references the section of the Internal Revenue Code (IRC) that contains the definition, rules and regulations that govern this category of tax-exempt organizations.

The IRS will grant 501(c)(3) status to an organization that completes the required application process, which includes the payment of fees. To apply for this federal tax-exempt status, an organization must first complete the process to become a nonprofit in its resident state or one of the U.S. territories. The nonprofit status is the prerequisite to applying for federal, tax-exempt status as a 501(c)(3).

The laws, process and fees for becoming a nonprofit vary slightly from state to state. However, the concept and operation of nonprofits are basically the same throughout the U.S.

A 501(c)(3) is an organization that has received special tax-exempt status from the federal government. This special status is what allows donors to make tax-deductible donations to the nonprofit. These organizations are defined as "charitable" by the IRS because they serve a public purpose by focusing on some "worthy cause." These charitable organizations provide a broad range of programs and services in the areas of education, science, arts & culture, employment, community development and other areas that bring some benefit to the public.

Every 501(c)(3) is a tax-exempt organization, but not every tax-exempt organization is classified as a 501(c)(3). The IRS has at least 35 different classifications for tax-exempt organizations. *The various types of organizations that may operate under tax-exempt status are listed on the following page.*

Most nonprofits evolve out of activities started by individuals or groups. At some point, it may be deemed more beneficial or necessary to establish a formal organizational structure. Of the numerous classifications of public and nonprofit organizations (i.e. school districts, churches, civics clubs, social clubs, trade associations), the 501(c)(3) is by far, the most utilized and recognized for the purposes of soliciting grant funds for community-based programs.

Although there is some distinction between a *501(c)(3) public benefit corporation* and a *nonprofit,* the following terms are often used interchangeably to describe a 501(c)(3): *nonprofit, not-for-profit, charity, or community based organization (CBO). Note: Non-Government Organization (NGO) is the term most commonly used in the international world of nonprofits.*

Table 6

IRS Subsection Codes for Tax-Exempt Organizations
(IRS Publication 557)

501(c)(1)	Corporations Organized under Act of Congress (including Federal Credit Unions)
501(c)(2)	Title Holding Corporation for Exempt Organization
501(c)(3)	Charitable Benefit Corporation (religious, educational, charitable, scientific, literary, testing for public safety, to foster national or international amateur sports competition, or prevention of cruelty to children or animals organizations)
501(c)(4)	Civic Leagues, Social Welfare Organizations, and Local Associations of Employees
501(c)(5)	Labor, Agricultural, and Horticultural Organizations
501(c)(6)	Business Leagues, Chambers of Commerce, Real Estate Boards, etc.
501(c)(7)	Social and Recreational Clubs
501(c)(8)	Fraternal Beneficiary Societies and Associations
501(c)(9)	Voluntary Employees Beneficiary Associations
501(c)(10)	Domestic Fraternal Societies and Associations
501(c)(11)	Teacher's Retirement Fund Associations
501(c)(12)	Benevolent Life Insurance Associations, Mutual Ditch or Irrigation Companies, Mutual or Cooperative Telephone Companies, Etc.
501(c)(13)	Cemetery Companies
501(c)(14)	State Chartered Credit Unions, Mutual Reserve Funds
501(c)(15)	Mutual Insurance Companies or Associations
501(c)(16)	Cooperative Organizations to Finance Crop Operations
501(c)(17)	Supplemental Unemployment Benefit Trusts
501(c)(18)	Employee Funded Pension Trust (created before June 25, 1959)
501(c)(19)	Post or Organization of Past or Present Members of the Armed Forces
501(c)(21)	Black Lung Benefit Trusts
501(c)(22)	Withdrawal Liability Payment Fund
501(c)(23)	Veterans Organizations (created before 1880)
501(c)(25)	Title Holding Corporations or Trusts with Multiple Parents
501(c)(26)	State-Sponsored Organization Providing Health Coverage for High-Risk Individuals
501(c)(27)	State-Sponsored Workers' Compensation Reinsurance Organization
501(c)(28)	National Railroad Retirement Investment Trust
501(d)	Religious and Apostolic Associations
501(e)	Cooperative Hospital Service Organizations
501(f)	Cooperative Service Organizations of Operating Educational Organizations
501(k)	Child Care Organizations
501(n)	Charitable Risk Pools
521(a)	Farmers' Cooperative Associations
4947(a)(1)	Non-Exempt Charitable Trusts
4947(a)(2)	Split-Interest Trust
170(c)(1)	Government Entity

"Nonprofit" Doesn't Mean "No Money"

"Nonprofit" doesn't mean that an organization can't generate revenue to cover its expenses, but it does mean that the activities must be designed and operated for the betterment or greater good of the community.

"Nonprofit" doesn't mean that an agency isn't allowed to have money remaining after all of its bills are paid. In the nonprofit world, the excess is called a "surplus" and within certain guidelines, may be used to support the ongoing activities of the organization. "Nonprofits" don't pay taxes on the surplus in the way that a "for-profit" or "profit" enterprise pays taxes on profits. However, nonprofits are responsible for payroll taxes for staff and other taxes associated with most business operations.

The following is a list of some of the most recognized and well-established, nonprofits in the United States:

American Cancer Society	Muscular Dystrophy Association
American Red Cross	Ronald McDonald House Charities
Boys & Girls Club(s)	Salvation Army
Boy Scouts of America	Tournament of Roses
Easter Seals	UNICEF
Goodwill Industries, Inc.	United Way
Kaiser Healthcare	Urban League
March of Dimes	YMCA's & YWCA's

Public schools and faith-based organizations are other categories of organizations that fall under the umbrella of tax-exempt, nonprofits.

What does a 501(c)(3) have to do with Grants?

Obtaining the 501(c)(3), charitable benefit status is the first eligibility requirement listed by funders for the overwhelming majority of grant applications. Some funders will award grants to organizations and groups that have a formal agreement with an established 501(c)(3) that serves as the nonprofit fiscal sponsor for the grant. A nonprofit fiscal sponsor assumes legal and fiduciary responsibility for the expenditure of grant funds (See pages 28 -30 for additional details).

<u>"Good Standing"</u>

A 501(c)(3) is considered in *good standing* if there are no current or pending financial, legal or programmatic improprieties. The status can be researched by:

1)   Contacting the department in your state capitol responsible for incorporating and overseeing nonprofit organizations. *This is usually the Secretary of State or the Department of Corporations.*

2)   Requesting a review of the most recent, audited financial statements from the nonprofit. The organization, Guidestar®, is a great resource. Their mission is: *"To revolutionize philanthropy and nonprofit practice by providing information that advances transparency, enables users to make better decisions, and encourages charitable giving."*

    Guidestar® gathers information on tax-exempt organizations from a variety of sources, including the IRS and nonprofit agencies. They maintain a database with this information. Some data is available free of charge. More detailed reports are available through paid subscription. Visit them at: www.guidestar.com

3)   Contacting funders who have provided support to the organization to gather feedback on their experience with the nonprofit. If the nonprofit has ongoing relationships with one or more funding sources, it is usually viewed as a positive reflection on their *standing.*

Note: Guidestar is also a useful grants research tool to review IRS Form 990's for foundation funders. You will be able to get details on the types of organizations and causes they support, including the amounts they have awarded to specific organizations.

What Purpose Does the 501(c)(3) Serve?

- Funding sources are extremely limited for grants that don't require 501(c)(3)'s. *(with the exception of public institutions like schools, parks, hospitals, etc.)*

- Awarding funds to a 501(c)(3) entitles corporations to deductions for charitable contributions.

- Foundations may jeopardize their legal status as tax-exempt charitable organizations if they award grants to organizations that don't have a 501(c)(3) or other eligible tax-exempt status (such as public schools and libraries, or faith-based organizations that operate non-sectarian programs for the general public).

- Tax-exempt status fulfills eligibility requirements to apply for many government and corporate grants.

- The tax-exempt status provides legal evidence that the organization has undergone a formal review progress to determine the legitimacy of its charitable purpose.

- The 501(c)(3) is the tax-exempt status that establishes organizational eligibility for grant consideration for government and foundation funders. The short list of exceptions includes public schools, colleges, faith-based organizations and some publicly-funded programs that seek grants (i.e. Parks & Recreation, Libraries).

> **Two options for nonprofits to pursue grants from the maximum number of sources possible:**
>
> 1) Set-up a 501(c)(3) <u>or</u>
>
> 2) Collaborate with an existing 501(c)(3)

How To Establish a 501(c)(3)

Laws that apply to nonprofits vary slightly from state to state; therefore it is important to follow the guidelines in your state. Federal IRS guidelines will apply to all nonprofits registered as 501(c)(3)'s.

The process is two-fold. Paperwork must be filed and fees submitted for both the state "nonprofit" and federal (IRS) "tax-exempt" designations. First, an organization is required to register as a nonprofit corporation in its resident state by filing Articles of Incorporation. Each state has its own unique numbering system for charitable organizations incorporated within its borders. The numbers that a state assigns to identify nonprofit organizations, reference the section of the state's Corporations Code or other applicable state regulations.

The basic process and paperwork to establish a 501(c)(3) nonprofit is summarized in the following bullet points. Additional details are available at www.irs.gov.

- Selection of corporate officers

- Articles of Incorporation
  (includes completion of an application and paying fees to the state in which the nonprofit is established)

- Prepare IRS Form 1023, Application for Recognition of Exemption. This will include the preparation of by-laws and other documents that must be submitted along with the completed application. By-laws are the set of written rules and regulations established by an association or corporation to provide a framework for how it will operate and manage its affairs.

- Submit completed application along with the required filing fees

Options to Establish 501(c)(3) Status or Affiliation

You can establish a 501(c)(3) status to meet the eligibility requirement in one of the following ways:

Option A: Hire An Attorney

Locate an attorney who has experience preparing and filing documents needed to obtain nonprofit and tax-exempt status for public benefit corporations. This is likely the most expensive route, but you will have the confidence that your documents and filings are being done properly. It will require the payment of fees for the attorney's services, plus the applicable filing fees for the state <u>and</u> federal applications. You can get a referral from a *nonprofit resource center* in your state (See page 50).

Option B: Nonprofit Fiscal Sponsorship

Become a member or affiliate of a 501(c)(3) that provides this type of program for community programs and organizations. This should always be more affordable than hiring an attorney. This arrangement provides a nonprofit group or organization with the ability to apply for grants. It will also allow your organization to provide receipts for donations received, which may be used by donors to qualify for tax-deductions.
If you don't have a relationship with a nonprofit that can serve as a fiscal sponsor for your programs, you can search for one at www.fiscalsponsordirectory.org. This online resource of fiscal sponsors throughout the U.S. is provided by the San Francisco Study Center.

Your program will have the benefits of the 501(c)(3) status. Also, the fiscal sponsor assumes fiduciary responsibility, which encompasses legal, financial and ethical duties. You will need to complete some type of application process, which may require an initial membership fee, plus a small percent of all funds raised by your organization.

Nonprofit fiscal sponsors usually charge a fee to cover the administrative expenses related to the financial and legal requirements they are required to maintain (i.e. recordkeeping and accounting, regular board meetings, preparation and filing of annual nonprofit tax returns). In exchange, your program will be able to conduct fundraising activities with the status as a tax-exempt, nonprofit program operating under the guidelines of the fiscal sponsor.

This arrangement also provides an opportunity for you to become knowledgeable about the basic policies and procedures involved in operating a 501(c)(3). It allows time to assess if it will be feasible to expend time and money to establish an independent nonprofit organization before expending time and money to form an independent nonprofit agency.

Option C: Establish a formal collaboration with an established 501(c)(3)

You may choose the option of having an existing nonprofit serve as the fiscal sponsor for your program. This method is very cost effective on the front end, as the only required investment is your time. You simply need to identify an established 501(c)(3) willing to form a collaborative partnership that can support your program. As long as your proposed activities are aligned their agency's mission and purpose, it will lay the groundwork for a successful nonprofit partnership. (Information on how to identify a nonprofit that may be appropriate for collaboration is included on pages 29 -32)

Option D: Do It Yourself

This method is recommended for those with a knack for "legalese" and familiarity with articles of incorporation and bylaws for nonprofit organizations. The out-of-pocket expenses will include filing fees for the state and federal applications, as well as the time and expenses invested to prepare all required documents.

You can use free online resources or purchase a workbook that includes detailed instructions and templates of the documents that have to be created.

Using Free Online Resources

State Application – for information and instructions to incorporate as a nonprofit in your state, logon to the homepage of your state's website. Look for *Secretary of State, Department of Corporations,* or *Corporations.* Locate the link for information on the required application process and fees for your state to establish a nonprofit.

Federal Application - Log onto the IRS homepage and "search" for Form 1023 (Application for Recognition of Exemption).   The link will provide access to detailed information on the application process, forms and fees.

Purchase A Workbook or Online Service

The most popular and widely used "do-it-yourself" workbooks on this subject are published by Nolo Press, Inc. (www.nolo.com). You can find additional resources by conducting a search on the internet.

Collaborate With An Existing 501(c)(3)

You may decide to postpone or eliminate the expense of forming your own nonprofit by collaborating (that is, establishing a formal agreement and working relationship) with an established nonprofit. The nonprofit should be located in the region where you plan to operate. Ideally, they should be located in, or have a history of providing programs in the same vicinity.

The most common collaboration will entail the nonprofit acting as the **fiscal agent** for your program/project. Grant checks are written to the organization that has the 501(c)(3) status, as they will be required to sign any grants awarded to your program. The fiscal sponsor must assume legal responsibility for ensuring that funds spent and activities conducted are in accordance with guidelines that govern nonprofits.

It is important for you and key person(s) at the 501(c)(3) to make joint decisions in advance about how the funding is to be identified, tracked and processed through their organization to operate your program. It is imperative to reach an agreement that includes specifics about what the sponsoring nonprofit will receive for their fiscal sponsorship and administrative oversight of your program.

The agreement may entail the payment of a percent or set amount of total funds raised by your organization. It may result in designing your program to include budget items in your grant request to pay the fiscal sponsor for time and resources they will need to provide to support your project (i.e. monthly rental fee, portion of salary for their receptionist who may provide some level of support for your program). The fiscal sponsor is required to include information about your grant activities in their financial reports and tax returns. Although you will need to prepare any reports required by funding sources for your activities, the nonprofit sponsor bears the ultimate responsibility for compliance with all grant agreements, including the assurance that you submit reports for your activities.

Exercise 2 on page 37 will be useful to help you identify potential nonprofits to approach regarding collaborating as your fiscal sponsor.

The following suggestions will be useful if you decide to take the collaboration route to work with a fiscal sponsor:

- Be thoughtful and honest with yourself about the compatibility of working with the fiscal sponsor.

- Their mission, goals and objectives must have some affinity with your existing or proposed program(s).

- Verify that the fiscal sponsor is in good financial and legal standing. (See page 24)

- Have a discussion about the process for terminating the relationship within a time frame that is reasonable, should it become necessary or desirable.

- Always put the details of the collaborative agreement in writing.

- Be sure to request documentation that indicates your collaborative agreement is approved by the Board of Directors of the 501(c)(3).

- Always prepare a written addendum or attachment to document any changes to the original agreement. Be sure to have it signed by both parties.

Questions to Ponder for Effective Collaboration

- *What is the mutual benefit?*
- *How can we leverage this relationship to maximize the benefits?*
- *How will we resolve challenges or disagreements?*

Written Collaborative Agreements

Different types of written agreements are used to establish collaborative partnerships between nonprofit organizations. This document describes the nature of the relationship of the participating organizations, basic parameters and what is expected of each one. It is important to remember that these agreements are legal and binding, so it is imperative to include details that will be important for the operation of your program.

It is best to draft an outline of the main points of concern for both parties prior to finalizing any agreement. Having a discussion to lay the groundwork for the business relationship between the parties, is one of the most important steps in the process.

> *Memorandum of Understanding*
> *"MOU" ("pronounce each letter")*
> *An MOU is the name commonly used to refer to these types of agreements.*

Once a general understanding has been reached on key points, a draft agreement should be typed and reviewed by you and the principal representative of the nonprofit for final additions, corrections, etc. After this has been completed, the final agreement should be revised, proofread and signed by both parties.

Having the document notarized is strongly recommended. Although the notary has no legal authority regarding the contents of the document, notarizing the document further validates the intentions and level of commitment on behalf of both parties.

The following pages contain an overview of MOU's, a sample agreement and a worksheet for preparing a basic MOU for a formal collaboration. The sample MOU is for a neighborhood group that needs a location to establish a community food pantry. In this example, the nonprofit organization providing the location will serve as the fiscal sponsor for the program.

Along with grant applications, some funders require the submission of MOU's to document agreements for nonprofit fiscal sponsorship and/or collaborative programming.

Four Common Types of Nonprofit Collaborative Arrangements

Table 7

TITLE	KEY POINTS
Collaborative Agreement	▪ Agreement between two or more organizations or programs ▪ A 501(c)(3) acts as the fiscal agent for another ("resident"*) program to solicit grant funds ▪ The 501(c)(3) has the legal responsibility for the funds solicited for the *resident** program, in accordance with all applicable laws governing nonprofits and tax-exempt organizations ▪ The resident program has a legal responsibility to uphold its end of the agreement with the 501(c)(3) fiscal sponsor
Memorandum of Understanding "M.O.U."	▪ Agreement between two or more organizations or programs ▪ Terms of the agreement dictate "who" is responsible for "what" ▪ This type of agreement is often used when there is no financial commitment that will result in an exchange of funds ▪ Some MOU's will include a financial commitment
Bilateral Agreement	▪ Agreement between a maximum of two organizations or programs ▪ Both parties have similar responsibilities and obligations ▪ May involve arrangement for an exchange of funds and/or services ▪ Each party bears a similar responsibility for maintaining the agreement
Letter of Support	▪ Prepared by 501(c)(3), agency or prominent community leader ▪ Sometimes included or required as a part of a grant proposal ▪ Demonstrates support for your project or program by the individual or group providing the letter ▪ This document does not establish a financial obligation on behalf of the supporter. It is simply an endorsement of support for the organization or project

*A resident program operates under the 501(c)(3) status of the host (fiscal sponsor) organization. The use of the term "resident" here is <u>not</u> related to the applicant organization's state of residence.

You should consult with an attorney to assure that your collaborative agreement is in compliance with applicable laws in your area and that all of the important issues that may impact your program have been addressed.

Memorandum of Understanding (MOU)

This agreement is between **ANOTHER SUPPER FOOD PANTRY (ASFP)** and the **MIDTOWN COMMUNITY CENTER (MCC)** for the twelve-month period from **APRIL 1, (Year____) thru MARCH 31, (Year _____).**

ANOTHER SUPPER FOOD PANTRY agrees to:

1. Solicit all funds and prepare grant applications for **AFSP** as a collaborative program of **MCC.**

2. Obtain and maintain all required licensing and insurance needed to operate the program, in accordance with federal, state and local laws.

3. Assume financial responsibility to have **MCC** included on all applicable insurance policies required to operate the program for the duration of this agreement.

4. Adhere to all **MCC** policies and procedures in the operation of the food pantry.

5. Cooperate with **MCC** staff in the development and implementation of procedures to ensure the most efficient operations possible.

6. Accept full financial responsibility for any damage to **MCC** equipment or facilities caused by food pantry staff, volunteers or clients.

7. Make grant proposals in-progress available for **MCC** personnel to review as appropriate.

8. Provide a monthly written report on the status of all grants and grant proposals.

9. Submit a detailed invoice to **MCC** for the distribution of funds awarded to, solicited by, or received on behalf of **ANOTHER SUPPER FOOD PANTRY** for all programs and services provided under, and related to this agreement.

10. Provide original receipts along with related invoices to **MCC** for all disbursement requests for expenditures.

11. List **MCC** as a major sponsor on the **AFSP** website, related social media tools, program materials (hardcopy and digital), and in press releases and media promotions.

MIDTOWN COMMUNITY CENTER (MCC) agrees to:

1. Act as the 501(c)(3) nonprofit fiscal sponsor for **ANOTHER SUPPER FOOD PANTRY (ASFP).**

2. Grant permission to **ASFP** to operate under the 501(c)(3) status of **MCC** to provide food, toiletry and other related items to individuals and families in the community.

3. Provide the kitchen facility and the adjacent storage area at no cost for the exclusive use of **ASFP** programs and activities.

4. Accept and deliver any and all **ASFP**-related correspondence to assigned **ASFP** personnel in a prompt manner.

5. Adhere to prompt follow-through in depositing funds awarded to or solicited by **ASFP**.

6. Maintain a separate accounting record to track all funds received and disbursed on behalf of **AFSP**, with an understanding that the executive director of **AFSP** is the sole designee authorized to approve requests and or expenditures submitted to **AFSP** for the processing of payments.

7. Adhere to prompt payment of all "cleared" funds awarded to, solicited by, or on behalf of **ASFP**.

Either party may cancel this agreement at anytime with an advance **90 DAYS** written notice. This will allow time to notify clients and coordinate a transition to another location or to refer clients to an alternative food program for low-income residents in the area.

Any modifications to this agreement must be in writing.

_____   _____

Fred Feeder, Director   DATE
ANOTHER SUPPER FOOD PANTRY
(ADDRESS)
(CITY, STATE, ZIP)

_____   _____

Dr. Hannah Helpful, Executive Director   DATE
MIDTOWN COMMUNITY CENTER
(ADDRESS)
(CITY, STATE, ZIP)

_____

Note: 1) Consult with an attorney experienced in nonprofits to ensure that your agreement is thorough and is in compliance with all applicable laws in your area.
2) If additional space is needed, prepare a separate page as an attachment to include the witness signatures and notary seal.

Memorandum of Understanding

This agreement is between **YOUR NAME** or **NAME OF PROGRAM** and **NAME OF EXISTING 501(C)(3)** for **TIME PERIOD** or **PROJECT TIMELINE.**

NAME OF PROJECT agrees to:

1. _____

2. _____

3. _____

4. _____

5. _____

EXISTING 501(C)(3) agrees to:

1. _____

2. _____

3. _____

4. _____

5. _____

Either party may cancel this agreement at anytime with an advance notice (i.e. **30 DAYS, WEEKS, MONTHS**). *The notice must include a brief outline of a proposed plan and timeline of at least **30/60/90** days to complete or phase out any portions of the project **currently in progress**).*

Each signature below attests to the mutual understanding of this agreement. Any modifications to this agreement must be in writing.

_____   _____
YOUR NAME, TITLE W/PROGRAM   DATE
NAME OF PROJECT/PROGRAM
ADDRESS

_____   _____
COLLABORATOR'S NAME, TITLE   DATE
NAME OF PROJECT/PROGRAM
ADDRESS

Steps To Take Until You Establish A 501(c)(3)

The number of funders that will award grants to individuals is extremely limited. The majority <u>do not</u> consider applications from organizations or programs that are not incorporated as 501(c)(3)'s.

That does not mean that you should not proceed with the operation of your program. You still have the option of collaborating with an existing nonprofit to serve as the fiscal sponsor. Some funders will award grants under this arrangement.

If you are already operating a program or providing services, you should gather and maintain detailed records on all activities and related income and expenditures as if you were already a nonprofit with a formal structure. If you are seeking funds for a project or program that is currently in existence or a project that has been completed, it is important to compile and organize the following categories of information (i.e. summer tutoring program, weekend neighborhood block parties, annual scholarship drive),

- Client information, including program registration forms and records, etc.

- Sign-in sheets for program activities

- Articles (online publications, blog posts, newspapers, newsletters, etc.)

- Audio & visual archives

- Flyers or pamphlets

- Letters of appreciation (participants, community, etc.)

- Receipts (be sure they are legible)

- Any other related information that can be documented

With this portfolio of your program's services and activities, you will be able to demonstrate that you have the ability to develop and implement a successful program. This is often the leverage that you need to show the program history that may be needed to obtain your first grant, independently or in collaboration with an established 501(c)(3). These materials will also provide you with useful information to outline and develop the organizational structure, program components and activities for your program.

Exercise 2 – Identify Potential Collaborators

Instructions: Complete the following chart with information on at least three (3) local nonprofit organizations that may be good prospects for you to approach to initiate a formal collaboration. It is important to identify potential partners with missions, programs or services that relate to your proposed collaboration.

Who? a) Name of Local Agency or Program *(include contact information)*	What Can They Do For You? b) What potential benefits can the collaborator bring to your program?	What Can You Do For Them? c) What potential benefits can your program bring to the collaborator?
1a) Contact person/info:	1b) 1c)	
2a) Contact person/info:	2b) 2c)	
3a) Contact person/info:	3b) 3c)	

37

HTTP://

Part II: Grant Research & Grant Applications

This section provides an overview of how to find information on grant opportunities and how to review grant guidelines to identify the most appropriate funding sources for your programs.

Upon the completion of Part II, you will be able to:

- Conduct grant research to find a variety of appropriate funding sources for your programs, including government agencies and foundation (corporate and private)

- Prepare a Letter of Intent (LOI) for a government funding opportunity

- Locate information and educational resources for nonprofit fundraising, including grant making and management

- Identify at least three funding sources most appropriate for your organization or programs

As you proceed with the completion of exercises in this workbook, concurrently it is important to begin the process of collecting and recording information onto the **Master Grant Data Worksheet** (Pages 180-231). If you will follow this recommendation, you will have all of the information needed to prepare any type of grant application by the time you complete this workbook.

Grant Research: Finding the Grant Sources

Whether you're looking for a specific funding source by name or simply searching for grant opportunities, you can find most of what you need on the internet. There are also a number of grant directories that offer memberships or monthly subscriptions and it is a good idea to become familiar with these resources. However, if you're willing to invest time, you will be able to locate most of what you need in exchange for the time spent online.

Most grant funding sources maintain websites where they publish their application guidelines. Whether they require hard copy or online submissions, the categories of information needed by most funders are the same.

Information and activities contained in the following sections on grant research are designed to teach you exactly what to look for, including:

- How and where to find funding sources appropriate for your programs,

- How to determine if your program is eligible,

- Whether the funding opportunity is the most appropriate for you to invest more time, and

- The information needed and the process to follow to apply.

As you begin to conduct research to learn about the grant application process, you'll become familiar with the categories of information that most funders include in their application guidelines, specifically:

- Mission, goals and objectives,

- Eligibility requirements for applicants,

- An overview of the application process,

- A list of previous grant awards,

- Answers to frequently asked questions (FAQ's), and

- Instructions on how to access a complete copy of the application

The categories of information and the application processes are basically the same for submitting grant requests via traditional hard copy or via an online application. Most online processes require the completion of an eligibility quiz in order to access the full application. The full application contains all of the questions and other items that will require a written response or additional documentation. An overview of online applications and e-applications, along with tips on how to access application questions starts on page 69.

Finding Grants On The Internet

If you have never conducted grant research, you will be surprised at the number of resources you will be able to locate in a matter of minutes. The majority of your time will be spent reviewing the information on all of the grants that you find. To provide ample time for an initial introduction to this process, a minimum of one hour is recommended for your first search. If your experience is typical, you will spend much more time than you thought as you discover an abundance of grant sources.

Before You Start - Internet Grant Research Tips*

1. You can find hundreds of funding resources, so be prepared to bookmark or take notes on the ones of interest to you. It is important to develop this habit as you conduct your research. This will ensure that you will capture and record the exact name of the funder or the web address for future reference.

2. If you're an old-school, hard copy die hard, don't go overboard printing every grant source that interests you. Reserve your printer cartridge for the ones that warrant an application.

3. For the ones you print, use notebooks or folders to organize the grants information either alphabetically, by funder name or by funding category (i.e. health, education, economic development, youth). This will make it easier for you to retrieve the information later.

Consider creating a "Grants Research" file by opening a blank word or text document that you can use to "cut & paste" pertinent information of interest to you from funders' websites.

---

*A digital filing system is recommended, however, tips for using hard copy files are included in this section.

Funding opportunities,

Grant opportunities,

RFP's, RFA's,

FOA's, NOFA's,

& more

Step-by-Step Grant Research On The Internet

This section introduces the steps to conduct research on the internet. A variety of terms are used to indicate the availability of grant funds. Be on the lookout for the terms noted in the dollar illustration at the bottom of the previous page.

When You Know The Name Of The Funding Source

If you know the actual name of the foundation or funding source, simply type it into the "search" box of your favorite search engine. If there is a website with that name, it should appear in the list displayed on your screen.

Examples: Target Foundation, Wells Fargo Foundation, Nissan Foundation

When You Don't Know The Name Of The Funding Source

If you don't know the actual name of the foundation or funding source, you can use your favorite internet search engine to locate thousands of potential funders by taking the following steps:

Locating Public and Foundation Grants

Step 1:   Type **"grants + foundations"**

Step 2:   Take a look at the list. Pay close attention to the brief descriptions and URL's (especially website addresses that align with names of foundations) and choose any of the resources that interest you. If the link leads you to a news story or announcement about a grant, look for the name of the funding source and perform a search to see if there is a website with information on their grant guidelines.

Narrow your search by keying in more specific information as indicated in the examples below:

Example A – To locate information on potential funding sources for youth programs in Nebraska, type **"grants + youth programs + Nebraska"**

Example B – To locate information on potential funding sources for senior services in Dallas, Texas, type **"grants + senior services + Dallas, TX"**

Example C – To locate information on potential funding sources for economic development projects, type **"grants + economic development + job training"**

Locating Corporate Grants

Some corporations have separate foundations that handle all of their charitable grantmaking activities. (i.e. Avon Foundation, Ben & Jerry's Foundation).

Some corporations process all of their charitable donations through specific departments or offices. The names of these departments will vary from company to company. To locate information on corporate grants, take the following steps:

Step 1: Type **name of the corporation** (Example: "Toyota")

Step 2: If the existence of a corporate foundation isn't readily apparent, look for department names similar to the ones in the list below:

charitable giving	community involvement	public support
charitable grants	community relations	foundations
community support	community contributions	philanthropy

Step 3: If you can't find anything on the site related to grants, contact their corporate office via e-mail or phone by clicking on the "CONTACT US" tab. The information is sometimes located on one of their webpages or in sections under the "About Us" or "Our Company" tab.

Make contact and ask for the person or division in charge of providing "support" for community programs. This individual will be able to let you know if the company offers grants. Some companies don't give grants, but they may donate products or services. If you ask them about grants, they may respond that they don't give grants and the conversation will end, without your having the opportunity to learn about other types of support available.

Be sure that your inquiry is a request regarding "support for community programs" so that you will have the opportunity to learn of "non cash" donations that might benefit your program.

Beware: Some funders clearly state a "Do not call" or "Do not contact us" policy. If this is the case, this directive will be noted in the grants section of their website or in their application guidelines. Other funders may welcome contact to discuss your proposed program or to answer questions about their application process. Whatever you do, be sure you do **not** contact any funder to ask a question that can be answered readily by conducting a careful review of their application guidelines, instructions and related information on their website. If you call or e-mail to ask for an answer that you would have found with a careful reading of their information, you run the risk of becoming a memorable potential applicant for all the wrong reasons. You always want to make a good first impression of your organization and program.

Exercise 3 – Locating Grants on the Internet: Corporate Giving

Instructions: Find and review grant applications and information from at least three corporate or foundation funders. Indicate at least one program category for which the funder provides grants. Choose corporations from the list below or include others of interest to you.

Ford Motor Corporation	Nissan Foundation	Hewlett-Packard Foundation
Ben & Jerry's Ice Cream	Northrop Foundation	The Grammy Foundation
Wells Fargo Foundation	Toyota Foundation	Nike Foundation

Corporate Funder #1: Name & Website	
Program/Funding Categories: (pertinent to your interest)	
Corporate Funder #2: Name & Website	
Program/Funding Categories: (pertinent to your interest)	
Corporate Funder #3: Name & Website	
Program/Funding Categories: (pertinent to your interest)	

Locating Government Grants

Most government entities that have grantmaking programs, including states, cities and other jurisdictions, maintain some type of centralized database of all grant opportunities.

The IRS issues the tax-exempt status and has oversight responsibilities for all nonprofit organizations in the U.S. and specified territories that fall under this category. This includes laws and standards for financial operations, recordkeeping and annual tax reporting. As a result, the standards and processes for grantmaking by the federal government, impact how grantmaking is done by all other categories of funders.

Federal Grant Funding Opportunities

The U.S. Government publishes all federal grant opportunities at: **http://grants.gov.** Contact offices of public and elected officials in your state, and local regions to request information on any upcoming federal grants that may be administered by their respective offices or departments.

It is very easy to locate information regarding grant opportunities at the federal level. "Grants.gov" is the one-stop shop to gain access to a database of more than 1,000 grant programs offered through the 26 federal grantmaking agencies noted in the following table. The grants are searchable by the type (category of funding) or by the specific federal agency.

Table 8

Federal Agencies with Grant Making Programs	
Agency for International Development	Department of State
Corporation for National and Community Service	Department of Transportation
Department of Agriculture	Department of the Treasury
Department of Commerce	Department of Veterans Affairs
Department of Defense	Environmental Protection Agency
Department of Education	Institute of Museum and Library Services
Department of Energy	National Aeronautics and Space Administration
Department of Health and Human Services	National Archives and Records Administration
Department of Homeland Security	National Endowment for the Arts
Department of Housing and Urban Development	National Endowment for the Humanities
Department of the Interior	National Science Foundation
Department of Justice	Small Business Administration
Department of Labor	Social Security Administration

The Grants.gov website is managed by the U.S. Department of Health and Human Services. The database is searchable in four different ways:

1. Name of federal agency (i.e. Department. of Education, Small Business Administration)
2. Funding Activity Category (i.e. Agriculture, Environment, Transportation)
3. Eligibility (type of applicant entity, i.e. Small Business, State Government, Nonprofit)
4. CFDA category (any of the 23 categories used by the "Catalog of Federal Domestic Assistance" to classify the type of project or activity identified for funding)

The majority of federal grants are available to organizations only. Opportunities for individuals are severely limited and are typically available only for arts and cultural programming. In many instances, the grants must still be awarded to a nonprofit organization, which acts as the fiscal sponsor on behalf of the individual who is receiving the grant award. One example is an "Artists-in-Residence" program that provides funding for an artist, musician or actor to work on a time-specific project while being paid by the host organization.

Each agency's website provides the official information on grant opportunities it offers. In addition, two federal sources provide this information:

Catalog of Federal Domestic Assistance (http://www.cfda.gov)*
*"The Catalog of Federal Domestic Assistance (CFDA) provides a full listing of all Federal programs available to State and local governments (including the District of Columbia); federally-recognized Indian tribal governments; territories (and possessions) of the United States; domestic public, quasi-public, and private profit and nonprofit organizations and institutions; specialized groups; and individuals. CFDA contains detailed program descriptions for more than 2,000 Federal assistance programs."

Federal Register (http://www.gpoaccess.gov/fr)*
*"Published by the Office of the Federal Register, National Archives and Records Administration (NARA), the Federal Register is the official daily publication for rules, proposed rules, and notices of Federal agencies and organizations, as well as executive orders and other presidential documents. It is updated daily by 6 a.m. and is published Monday through Friday, except Federal holidays. This online resource contains Federal Register volumes from 59 (1994) to the present."

Some federal grant funds are administered by state and county governments. In these instances, the respective state or local government agency is responsible for coordinating the grantmaking process, including the oversight of all programs and projects funded. Similar to Grants.gov, some states, counties and cities have websites that serve as central clearinghouses for their grant opportunities. It is important to contact the offices of federal, state or local officials in your region to get information on where and how to access information on current and future funding opportunities.

Federal

You will need to register or sign-in with the name and Employer Identification Number (E.I.N.) of your nonprofit to apply for funding at **http://grants.gov**.

If your program will operate under a fiscal sponsor, you will need to obtain their permission to either:

1) Use their sign-in information or
2) Create a login account using their information. It is imperative to obtain written permission. This can be accomplished by an e-mail exchange with the fiscal sponsor's executive director (or other authorized designee) that clearly documents your request for permission, and most importantly, their authorization. The application will need to be submitted under the name of the fiscal sponsor, but the application will include details and budget information for your specific program.

State

Unless your state has a centralized grants database similar to what is available at the federal level, grant opportunities will be announced by specific departments. Grant funding opportunities will be announced through an RFA, RFP or similar process.

You should identity all departments in your state that offer funding for activities most closely aligned with the program that you wish to have funded. Once you identify potential matches, check the appropriate websites or call the specific state offices (i.e. Arts Council, Education Department, Forestry and Lakes Management). If information on grant opportunities is readily available, locate the **Search** box on the funder's website and type a word or phrase similar to the following: "grants," "funding opportunities," "RFP's," "RFA's," etc.

Local & Regional

It is important to become familiar with the government structure in your community and surrounding region. This may help you identify departments and agencies with grantmaking programs. The internet makes it easy to conduct research for most government grants. Remember, since government agencies provide grants funded by public dollars, they have an obligation to publicize the opportunities to ensure that eligible organizations within respective funding categories are informed and afforded the opportunity to apply. One of the easiest ways for them to satisfy this requirement is by posting funding opportunities on their websites and using social media. They may also distribute announcements to their e-mail and mailing lists, as well as disseminating information at community events through traditional media outlets.

> *Always check each website you visit during your grant research to see if there is an option to register to receive e-notifications of upcoming funding opportunities.*

<u>State & Local</u>

Some jurisdictions have also established web pages to post all grant opportunities. This information can be obtained by contacting the office of public officials in your area. You can find contact information for public officials in the government section of your local telephone directory or on the websites of elected (or appointed) officials and government offices in your region.

If you have interest in a grant from a particular office, you can obtain information by visiting their website or calling (i.e. Parks & Recreation, Public Health Department, Housing Department). If you want to find out if certain offices issue announcements for funding opportunities, contact them directly to make an inquiry.

Exercise 4 – Locating Grants on the Internet: Government Grants

Instructions: Log onto the website of a federal, state or local government agency and locate at least three funding sources for one or more of the nine program categories listed below. You may choose other program areas of interest to you as well.

Education	Transportation	Parks & Recreation
Health	Senior Services	Economic Development
Arts	Fire & Safety	Energy Efficiency

1.	Type of Program: _____

	Gov't. Dept. or Agency: _____

	Web address: _____

2.	Type of Program: _____

	Gov't. Dept. or Agency: _____

	Web address: _____

3.	Type of Program: _____

	Gov't. Dept. or Agency: _____

	Web address: _____

Locating Other Grant Resources

Government (federal, state, regional, and local)

Once you understand how public funds flow through various departments at the federal, state and local levels, it is easy to get information on grant opportunities. Usually a careful review of the respective department's website will provide information on current and upcoming funding opportunities. If no grant information is posted, you can use their "Contact Us" link to make an inquiry via e-mail or phone.

Departments and divisions of the government are required by law to provide the public with information regarding opportunities for grants and other government contracts for goods and services. The goal is to ensure that all eligible applicants have access to information about grant opportunities. Information on government grants can be obtained in the following ways:

1.	Department websites: Government offices that administer grants, post information on their websites. They also publish announcements of grant opportunities in national, regional and local newspapers as appropriate for the specific funding opportunity. They may also distribute the information to a list that is limited to certain categories of potential applicants (i.e. RFP announcement regarding youth obesity prevention may be sent to all elementary schools and community health clinics within a certain region that serve families with children).

2.	Department announcements: All government departments that provide grant funds are required to post information in a manner that is accessible to the public. They typically post announcements on bulletin boards located in their offices and distribute information to their constituents via e-mail, regular mail and at community events.

3.	Request to be placed on mailing list(s): Once you have determined that a particular government office has grant funds that may be of interest, you can request to be placed on their e-mail (or hard copy) list to receive notices of upcoming applications.

4.	Classified advertisements: Traditionally, government agencies have placed advertisements in newspapers to announce funding opportunities. This practice is still in effect, with the announcements usually found in the Classifieds section of regional or local newspapers. Information on bidding and contracting opportunities will be found in the same section, usually near the front or near the back of the Classifieds section.

Note: An increasing number of funders have adopted the internet and other digital media as their primary mode of communicating information about their grantmaking opportunities. The use of traditional channels like hard copy mailings and classified ads in print publications continues to decrease.

Corporations & Foundations

Paying attention to news stories about charitable donations and grants awarded to organizations may prove beneficial to locating funders appropriate for your programs. Use a search engine to identify potential funding sources using the following:

- News articles that feature stories about donations to community groups by certain corporations or foundations.

- News articles that announce a period of huge profits for a corporation that has a history of supporting community programs. Timely research on their website may enable you to gather application information or to identify the individual or department responsible for providing community support

Nonprofit Industry Grant Resources

The nonprofit sector has a wealth of publications, associations and organizations that provide information on funding opportunities. Organizations that specialize in providing professional training resources and information on nonprofit management are located throughout the United States.

Commonly referred to as **nonprofit resource centers** or **nonprofit libraries**, each of these organizations operates independently and may be identified by a variety of names, including: Nonprofit Resource Centers, Philanthropy Libraries and Volunteer Centers. Some have names that provide little indication of their roles as information hubs for grant opportunities.

Those that meet criteria established by the New York-based, Foundation Center are designated as "**Cooperating Collections.**" They provide free information and maintain a collection of current publications produced by the Foundation Center, as well as other educational materials to learn how to start, fund and management nonprofits.

Open to the public, each organization maintains its own schedule of workshops on nonprofit topics, including grantmaking. All of these organizations provide some services free-of-charge, however they also offer services that may require a registration or participation fee. Like any other organization, they have to cover expenses to maintain and staff these nonprofit community resources.

These centers are also an excellent resource to get referrals for professionals with expertise in the nonprofit sector, including attorneys, bookkeepers and other consultants. They often host regular networking events to convene executive directors and other staff from local nonprofits. These activities are excellent opportunities for grant writers to pursue employment or market their services as consultants.

To locate organizations that provide resources and training materials for fundraising and management in the nonprofit sector, use an internet search engine to request information for your geographic region of interest. The following are provided as examples of what to type:

- "Name of State/Region, Nonprofit Center" (Example: "Texas, nonprofit center")

- "Name of State/Region, Nonprofit Library" (Example: "Ohio, nonprofit library")

Three nationally-recognized grant resources that have an online presence, as well as printed publications include:

- The Foundation Center (**www.foundationcenter.org**)
  This organization maintains a database of foundation funding sources. A choice of subscription packages is available to provide detailed information and contact information for approximately 100,000 foundation funders.

- The Chronicle of Philanthropy (**www.philanthropy.com**)
  Based in Washington, D.C., this bi-weekly publication provides information on the nonprofit sector and includes listings of grant opportunities in each issue.

- The Grantsmanship Center (**www.tgci.com**)
  This organization conducts grant writing trainings throughout the U.S. and maintains a database that includes government grant opportunities.

Correspondence Related to Grant Applications

All funding sources provide written information on their eligibility requirements, guidelines and process for grant requests. Once you're familiar with where to look for grants, getting application information is a simple process.

All government grants have application deadlines. Many foundations have application deadlines, but some accept applications year-round.

Letter of Intent (LOI) for Government Grants

Government grant applications sometimes require an applicant to submit a Letter of Intent (LOI) during a specific time period, prior to submitting the application. A *Notice of Intent to Apply* is another name synonymous with an LOI for a government funder. An LOI always has a deadline that precedes the grant application deadline. This timeline may span anywhere from about two (2) weeks to ten (10) weeks prior to the application due date, based on the funder

A funder may require this step for all applicants who plan to submit proposals in order to confirm that a potential applicant is eligible and that the proposed program is aligned with funding priorities. The LOI also provides the funder with information regarding the geographic location of applicants. The funder may use this information to conduct additional outreach to encourage applications from areas and target populations not adequately represented in the pool of LOI's submitted.

The government agency will provide instructions for a *Letter of Intent* if it is required. The following categories of information are usually requested:

1)   Name of organization,
2)   Name or type of program,
3)   Target populations,
4)   Geographic service area,
5)   Funding category (if applicable, a list of options will be provided), and
6)   Amount requested

A funder may request an LOI online, faxed, or via mail in hardcopy format. If an online LOI is required, instructions will be provided on the funder's website.

Two samples are provided for your review on the following page.

Note: LOI's for corporate and foundation funders serve a different purpose and require more detail. Samples prepared for government funders are introduced on page 53. A sample of format appropriate for a foundation or corporate funder, along with a program budget, is provided on pages 57-60.

> *Government agencies may use a unique numbering system to assign an identity to specific grant projects.*
>
> *Examples: RFP 268-12: Youth Initiative <u>or</u>*
> *RFP 07382-2020: Senior Services*

Samples of Hardcopy LOI's for Government Grants

(SAMPLE A)
Letter of Intent

(DATE)

(FUNDING SOURCE)
(ADDRESS)
(CITY, STATE, ZIP)

SUBJECT: Letter of Intent to Apply for Funding – Youth Services
           RFP #02-3459

Dear (CONTACT):

Youth Opportunity, Inc., a 501(c)(3), will be submitting an application for antiviolence services under RFP #02-3459.

Sincerely,

Danny Young
Youth Services Coordinator

(SAMPLE B)
Letter of Intent

(DATE)

(FUNDING SOURCE)
(ADDRESS)
(CITY, STATE, ZIP)

SUBJECT: *Letter of Intent to Apply for Funding*
           Department of Mental Health Services
           Outpatient Services – RFP #01-287739-A

Dear (FUNDING SOURCE):

Community Counseling Services, Inc., a 501(c)(3), will be submitting an application with a request for $160,000 for outpatient services for low-income women and children who reside in the northwest region in Jeff Davis County.

Sincerely,

Sally Psych
Director of Counseling Services

LOI's and LOA's for Corporations and Foundations

For **non-government** funders like for-profit corporations and foundations, an **LOI** usually refers to a **Letter of Interest** *or* **Letter of Inquiry**. This type of LOI typically requires more detail than an LOI for a government funder.

> **Non-government funders use LOI's to prescreen potential applicants to determine if an invitation will be extended to accept a full proposal.**

In some limited cases, a non-government funder may regard the LOI as an application. If so, this will be noted in their instructions.

> **Reminder: For a government funder, a Letter of Intent (LOI) is used as notification of an applicant's intent to apply for a specific funding opportunity.**

An **LOA** is a **Letter of Application**. Although the term is sometimes used interchangeably with the LOI, some funders request it in lieu of a standard application or proposal.

Some corporate and foundation funding sources require a *Letter of Request or Letter of Application* from a perspective grantee as a first step. An LOR or LOA serves the same purpose as a grant application. Either document may serve as the _first_ step or as the only step in the application process. Typically, the funding source will provide some guidelines and may request a specific format for preparing the *Letter*. Instructions will be provided for LOI's that have to be prepared and submitted online.

An LOI or LOA prepared in a hard copy format is usually two to three pages maximum and includes details and highlights of your organization and program. Prior to the advent of the internet, these documents were routinely referred to as "mini-proposals" since they include the basic elements of a full proposal. The funder may provide instructions to guide you in preparing an LOI or LOA. The table on the following page provides an overview of the purpose served by LOI's and LOA's.

Purpose for the Letter of Interest or Letter of Application

Table 9

What do LOI's/LOA's do for the funding source?	What do LOI's/LOA's do for the applicant?*
Assists in assessing how closely your proposed project/program fits their general or specific criteria for funding consideration.	Serves as a guideline for writing a more detailed proposal that may be required by the funding source.
May prompt a funder to send you an "invitation" to apply; this process is used by some funders to streamline their process of accepting and reviewing applications that will be considered for a grant award.	Can be used as a template for writing future grant proposals.
May require that you indicate the amount of money that you plan to request for your project/program.	Each *Letter* that you prepare provides additional experience in proposal development and grant writing.
*When the LOA is the only document requested by a funder, they will review it and make a decision to either award or decline your request.	

Additional information about LOI's and LOA's for corporation and foundation funders is provided on the next page, followed by a sample letter that includes a summary budget.

LOI's and LOA's provide corporate and private foundations with an overview of your organization and proposed program. Attachments that include supplemental information may also be required. This information enables them to determine if your request fits within the scope of their objectives. If the funder uses these documents as part of an initial screening process and wishes to give a request more consideration, they may extend an invitation for the applicant to submit a full proposal or application. At this point the applicant will receive additional information, including instructions on how to access an online application that may require a password.

> **For some corporate and foundation funders, the *Letter of Request* serves as the grant application.**

In other instances, a separate application is required along with attachments noted in the instructions. Some funders accept online applications only. Some use a hybrid application process that may require an application to be downloaded, prepared on hardcopy forms and submitted through regular mail. Others accept hard copy applications only.

Some funding sources don't provide standard application forms. Therefore, it is important to know what to include in the LOI. In addition to including key categories of information found in most proposals, it is important to communicate the most important and impressive things about the proposed program, project or activity to the funder.

A sample of a three-page LOI for a corporate or private foundation begins on the following page. The accompanying program budget is included.

> ## Two Grant Writing Tidbits...
>
> *...The number of funders using the hardcopy application process is steadily decreasing.*
>
> *...LOI's*, LOA's and LOR's are terms sometimes used interchangeably.*
>
> **Not applicable to LOI's for government funders.*

An overview of common responses to LOI's by funders is provided on page 61.

Letter of Interest/Inquiry/Application

(DATE)

Grants Administrator
U.S. Funding Foundation
7389 Money Way
Los Angeles, CA 90008

Letter of Interest

Dear Grants Administrator:

We hope to be considered for grant funds in the amount of $16,000 to establish a tutoring program to complement our after school performing arts/dance program. Students from low-income households will benefit from structured, educational services provided by graduate students completing internships at the local university.

Organizational Overview

Dancing Shoes is a 501(c)(3) that operates a tap, jazz and ballet dance program for youth in Long Beach, CA. More than 200 elementary school children have participated in this program since it was launched 18 months ago. Boys and girls from three local public schools are recruited to participate at the beginning of each school year.

We are in need of funds to expand our programming to include tutoring in math, English and reading for youth who attend the "Dancing After School" program. The grades of students who participate throughout the school year have improved overall. Biannual recitals are held to showcase the artistic talents and academic achievements of these children.

When compared to children in the same age/grade group, standard test scores in reading, comprehension and math are an average of 25% or one grade higher among children in this program. In addition, participants have a lower overall rate of incidents related to disciplinary actions for behavioral problems.

Located in a community described as low-income, many of our students are considered "latch key" kids and would greatly benefit from the proposed, one-hour tutoring session that takes place on-site prior to the two-hour dance class. The lack of structured, after-school programs places these children at risk for recruitment or harassment by local gang members and other negative influences in the community.

Proposed Program

We have a collaborative agreement with a local university to provide five tutors per week for this program. The tutors provide one-on-one and small group tutoring Mondays through Thursdays from 4 p.m. to 7 p.m. The chair of their English Department will coordinate the recruitment of graduate students who are pursuing teaching credentials. Each will receive course credit for completing a 12-week tutoring assignment.

Children enrolled in the program are in grades 1 thru 6. More than 90% of them attend Briarway Elementary, the local public school. The remaining 10% attend public and private schools in surrounding communities.

Target Population

Our program is located in a census tract defined as low-income by the U.S. Bureau of Statistics. The average per capita income is estimated at 200% of the Federal Poverty Level. We estimate approximately 70% are low-income. This figure is based on the number of students who participate in the Federal Lunch Program at school, a commonly cited indicator of economic status.

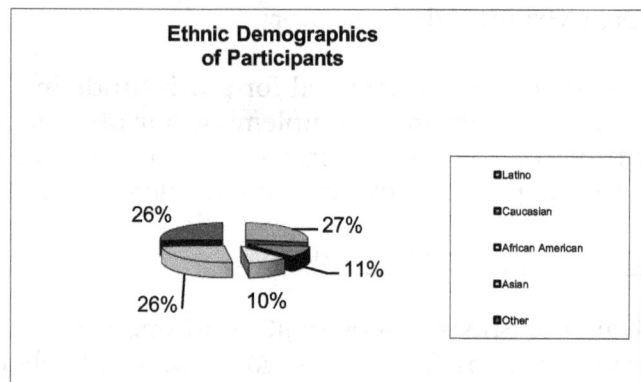

Ethnic Demographics of Participants

- Latino
- Caucasian
- African American
- Asian
- Other

27%
11%
10%
26%
26%

Data from the local school district reflects that 17% of the children live in foster homes and up to 40% live in a home headed by a single-parent home (primarily single mothers with no formal education or skills to be competitive in the local economy).

Children who reside in the community are faced with the unfortunate challenges of high-crime, higher-than-average teen pregnancy rates, high-unemployment and routine violence among local, rival gangs.

Needs Assessment & Evaluation

The high school dropout rate in this community is almost twice the state average. Research by the U.S. Department of Education indicates that poor performance in elementary and middle school has a direct impact on high school dropout and graduation rates. Programs like this have been shown to have a positive impact on educational outcomes in communities described as low-income.

Pretests will be administered upon enrollment to determine each student's academic levels. The Program Coordinator will monitor the progress of participants on an ongoing basis. Attendance records and assignments completed with the tutor(s) will be reviewed, along with interim progress reports and report cards. Post-tests will be administered at the end of each subject module to measure improvement in each area. This information will be used to make program adjustments for individual students and for the entire program as needed.

Use of Funds

The total budget for this after school program is $37,350. A grant from the U.S. Funding Foundation will be used for the following expenses:*

Program Coordinator (part-time)	$ 5,000
Educational supplies	3,000
Multimedia equipment	2,000
Printing/Copying	1,000
Outreach/Advertising	2,000
Books/Magazine Subscriptions	1,800
Mileage Reimbursement (for tutors)	1,200
	$16,000

Please contact me if you need any additional information.

Sincerely,

Tony Tapper
Program Coordinator
(123) 456-789
tonytap@bop.com

Enclosure: Copy of IRS Determination Letter – Proof of 501(c)(3)
                Board of Directors List

The $16,000 budget above is specific to amount requested in this sample LOI. It includes a list of line items for which this specific grant would be used if awarded. The full program budget of $37,350 is provided on the following page.

After School Program (Tutoring & Dance) Program Budget	
Personnel	
Program Coordinator (.25 FTE*)	$12,500
Administrative Assistant (.10 FTE*)	3,000
Personnel Subtotal	**$15,000**
Payroll Taxes & Benefits (30%)	4,500
Total Personnel	**$19,500**
Operating Expenses	
Educational Supplies	**$3,000**
Facility Maintenance	1,200
Multimedia Equipment	2,000
Refreshments/Snacks	2,400
Printing/Copying	1,000
Outreach/Advertising	3,000
Books/Magazine Subscriptions	1,800
Mileage (for tutors)	1,500
Total Operating Expenses	**$15,900**
Administrative Overhead (10% of Personnel)	1,950
Total Program Budget	**$37,350**

*See page 132 for the definition and overview of FTE's

Funder Responses to LOI's

After you submit your *LOI*, you can expect a response similar to one of the following from the funding source, typically in the form of an e-mail or letter.

1. ..."We have received your application. Our grant review panel will be meeting at the end of this quarter. You will be notified in the event that your proposal is chosen for funding."

    Simply be patient and hope for good news.

2. ..."Unfortunately, your proposal has not been selected for funding ..."

    It's not personal! This is probably their standard "decline letter" and they rarely provide specific reasons. It's usually because there were too many requests for the grant funds they had available. Check to see when you will be able to apply to this funder again in the future. Unless the funder expresses they do not wish to be contacted, call or e-mail to ask if they are willing to share what you could have done to make your proposal more competitive. Be sure to ask when you will be eligible to apply again. If they provide feedback, use the information to strengthen all of your future proposals.

3. ..."We need additional (specific) information in order to consider your proposal"
    <u>or</u>

    This could possibly mean good news at some point in the future. Be grateful you didn't get Response #1 above. At least you're still in the running. Follow up with an immediate response to provide them with the information, or inform them of exactly how quickly you will provide the requested information. Then, get busy to make good with the delivery of a prompt and complete response.

4. ..."Congratulations, your proposal has been recommended for funding."

    Hallelujah! They're about to "Show You The Money!" Respond with an immediate "Thank You!" If they called you, call and thank them, then immediately send an additional thank you via e-mail or personal letter. They will inform you of the process required to receive the grant award. Be sure to follow-up on any instructions provided in a timely manner.

Part III: Reviewing Grant Applications

This section provides instructions on what to look for to identify funding opportunities best suited for your programs. It also provides instructions on how to develop a plan and detailed outline that will make it easy to respond to any item requested on a grant application.

Upon the completion of Part III, you will be able to:

- Conduct a quick review of an application to determine if it warrants an investment of more time

- Review an application thoroughly to identify the key points and objectives that relate to your program(s).

- Identify the different types of online and hard copy grant application processes

- Prepare a detailed outline that includes a complete list of all grant application questions posed by a funder. This outline will be used to prepare all of the details to develop your completed proposal

- List the ten most common categories of information requested on grant applications, as well as the attachments most commonly required

As you proceed with the completion of exercises in this workbook, concurrently it is important to begin the process of collecting and recording information onto the **Master Grant Data Worksheet** (Pages 180-231). If you will follow this recommendation, you will have all of the information needed to prepare any type of grant application by the time you complete this workbook.

Overview of Grant Applications

The grant application is the starting point to prepare a formal request to submit to a funder. The term "grant application" may be used to refer to the set of questions and any forms that require written responses from a perspective applicant. The term is also used to refer to the completed application or proposal submitted to a funder. For the purposes of this section, the term "grant application" refers to the set of guidelines, questions, as well as any forms provided by a funding source that need to be completed and submitted along with the grant request.

Grant applications provide the framework for all of the information and documents that have to be compiled or created to submit a funding request. The specific questions, process and format for applications will vary from funder to funder, however, there are certain categories of information that all funders require.

Think of the application guidelines as your blueprint to prepare for and build your formal request for grant funding. The Grantbuilder™ System includes a tool that makes is easy to conduct a thorough review of any grant application. Once completed, the **Grant Application Review Worksheet** introduced on pages 76-77 is useful for a number of purposes:

1) Completing the worksheet requires the grantwriter to learn important information about the funder and to record details about what the funder requires of all grant applicants,

2) It provides enough information to determine if a specific funding source is appropriate for an organization to proceed with the application, and

3) Creates a summary reference sheet for a funder that can be filed for convenient retrieval, updating and reference in the future.

Basics of Reviewing Grant Guidelines and Applications

Application instructions may range from a one-page document that takes a few minutes to review, to multiple pages that may take hours to decipher. Once you select applications that seem appropriate for your program, it is important to get answers to a number of questions right away. Not every application will address all of these questions, but many of them will be answered by a careful review of application materials: (The Grant Application Review Worksheet introduced on pages 76-77 can be used for this purpose.) As you become familiar with applications from different funders, you will become more skilled in getting answers to these questions quickly and easily.

Questions	Why You Need To Know
1. Is there an application deadline?	*This will determine if there is enough time to prepare and submit the application.*
2. Other important timelines? • Funder's grant review schedule • Projected date(s) for funder to announce and distribute grants	*This information is useful for formulating your overall fundraising plan for your project and for coordinating the application with other potential funding sources within designated time frames.*
3. Contact information? (person's name and job title, mailing address, e-mail address, etc.)	*If a phone number or e-mail address is provided, it may come in handy if you have questions; in the event of a tight turnaround time to meet a deadline for a hard copy submission, it will be important to have the street address in case you need to deliver it in person or ship it overnight.*
4. Funder's mission and objectives?	*Provides you with an overview of how your program might align with their mission.*
5. Do they provide information on similar programs they've funded in the past? If so, Who was funded? Where? How much? What types of programs?	*Gives you a clear picture of the types of organizations and programs they like to fund and the amounts/ranges they give to various types of projects.*
6. Do they fund the specific type of program, project or activity that you have in mind?	*An indicator of whether or not your program may be given serious consideration.*
7. Do they fund programs in your geographic region?	*Determines if your program is in a region where they're likely to consider funding*

Questions	Why You Need To Know
8. Does your 501(c)(3) have to be in existence for a minimum period of time to qualify for funding?	*If their application requests financial statements for the past two years, it is an indication that the organization is expected to have been in existence for at least that period of time.*
9. Does the 501(c)(3) have to have a *minimum* or *maximum* budget to qualify for funding?	*Gives you a clear indication of whether they fund start-up, small, mid-sized or large, well-established organizations.*
10. Do they require *matching funds*? If so, is a cash match required or are *inkind** (donated) goods and services acceptable?	*Lets you know how much cash or other resources you will need to raise for a program to meet the funder's criteria.*
11. Do they require or recommend *letters of support* or collaborations with other local organizations?	*Indication that funder may expect you to leverage your resources with those of one or more existing groups or organizations.*
12. Do you need to gather any additional attachments, data, etc?	*Provides information to determine if you will be able to provide (create or access) the requested items within the timeline.*
13. Do you need to submit any graphic or audiovisual materials?	*Same as #12 above.*
14. Do they require a standard application form, LOI or full proposal?	*Helps you to determine the amount of content to prepare to fit within the required format (online, standard forms, hardcopy).*
15. Do they have specific funding categories?	*Determines if your program fits into one or more of their funding categories to maximize your chances for funding consideration.*
16. Do they provide "one-time" or "multi-year" funding?	*Helps you design your program and budget appropriately for the funding request*
17. **Specific to arts grants:** You will need to provide samples of your work. What are their specifications?	*They may request a link to a website or other online source to view your work sample(s). If they require the submission of samples, they will let you know their preferred file format and whether to attach the file(s) with an online application or to submit a CD, DVD or other storage media.*

Once you've obtained the answers to these important questions, you can make informed decisions about the most appropriate application(s) to prepare for your program

*See page 134 for the definition and examples of "inkind" resources.

Grant Application Basics

The terms *application* and *proposal* are used interchangeably. The internet has revolutionized the grant writing process since the mid-1990's. Although some funders still use *hard copy* applications, this traditional format is rapidly being replaced by the use of online applications.

Some funders use a *hybrid system* that may require the applicant to complete some portion of the application online, with a requirement to mail or deliver hard copies of certain documents.

An introduction to online applications is provided in the section below. A more detailed overview is included on pages 69-72. However, the process to gather and prepare the contents for all grant applications is the same, online or hard copy.

Most hard copy grant proposals will range from three to fifteen pages of narrative, excluding the budget and other attachments. Proposals for large-scale projects can be 50, 100, 200 pages or more (i.e. facility construction that requires copies of permits, copies of architectural renderings; regional health clinic collaboration that requires documents from all participating organizations).

Online Applications & E-Applications

An increasing number of funders use some type of online application process. This method is expected to replace the use of hard copy versions for most funders at some point in the future. It is important to make the distinction between a funder providing their application information on line, as opposed to providing a way for their application to be completed and submitted through an online system.

An E-Application (E-app) is the type of online application that can be prepared and submitted in its entirety online via an application specifically designed for this purpose. The use of data fields to record information is another distinction of e-apps. These data fields (or boxes) require the applicant to enter information in response to questions on the application.

All online application systems include guidelines and instructions that are usually easy to follow. Additional information and instructions for using online applications and e-applications are included on pages 69-72.

Standard Application Form(s)

Some funders provide one or more forms that may be in e-app or hard copy format. Forms include instructions, some more detailed than others. Sometimes, an *Application Cover Sheet* provided by the funder, is the only standard form provided, with the remainder of the proposal prepared as a narrative in response to a set of questions. Some funders provide a set of forms that require typed responses. The set of forms may comprise the entire proposal, or it may require the preparation of a separate narrative and budgets using software like MS Office®. Attachments may be required.

Letter of Application (LOA) or LOI

Most funders provide instructions on what to include in an LOA in terms of content and maximum page length. The most common length is two to five pages* and may require additional attachments (i.e. budget sheets, IRS letter to verify tax-exempt status). For funders that don't provide specific instructions, it is important to know what information to include. The ten most common items to include are introduced on page 74.

Multi-Page Proposal

Some proposals require a combination of standard forms provided by the funder, along with attachments to provide details about your agency or program. Proposals may range from a few pages to several hundred, depending upon the funder and the type of request.

Proposals that exceed thirty pages are typically prepared for projects that require extensive documentation (i.e. construction grants that require architectural renderings, building permits, financing documents; research grants that require curriculum vitae of principal researchers that will be involved on the project and a copy of the applicant's research protocol). This includes government grants with requests for large, multi-agency projects or foundation grants that provide funds for capital campaigns, such as construction projects.

———————————————

*Applicable to an LOI that serves as the grant application.

<u>Online Applications</u>

Online applications can be completed, reviewed and submitted online in their entirety or as part of a hybrid application that also requires the submission of hard copy documents. It is important to make a distinction between applications that can be prepared and submitted entirely online, in contrast to hybrid formats. The term "online applications" may refer to a system that requires applicants to complete forms online that must be downloaded, printed and sent by mail or other delivery method.

This workbook uses the term online application to refer to a grantmaking software system that allows the applicant to complete the entire process through a funder's website. No hard copies are required. This type of online application is designed with data fields that require the applicant to type or "cut & paste" information into the application. This type of software supports the online submission of an electronic application (e-application) and all required attachments.

The terms online application and e-application are often used interchangeably. However, it is important to understand the distinctions. There are two major types of online applications as described below:

1.   E-Applications

E-Applications use grantmaking software that has been customized for the funder. Think of it as a special website where an applicant can prepare and submit the entire application, including all required attachments. An e-application is a type of online application. Some require the applicant to create a login name and password to access the application. This will require the use of an email address, which the online system will use to send auto-replies and additional instructions. The email address may also serve as the username.

Most require a potential applicant to complete a brief online **eligibility quiz**. The quiz is comprised of a series of questions to help the potential applicant determine whether its organization and proposed project meet the funder's criteria. Many of the questions require a "yes" or "no" response. Some require specific information related to your organization or program. Your response will determine if you will be allowed to continue to the next part of the application, or it will provide an auto-response that you are not eligible. Some of the most common questions found on eligibility quizzes for e-apps are listed below:

- Is your organization a registered 501(c)(3)?
- What is your organization's EIN? (employer identification number)*
- Is your organization located in a particular city, congressional district or other designated area?
- What percent of your clients are low-income?
- Is your request for a fundraising event or other non-program purpose?

E-apps typically provide a field for the applicant to type in the nonprofit's federal employee identification number (EIN). An EIN serves as the tax identification number for the 501(c)(3), similar to a social security number for an individual taxpayer.

This is a small sampling of questions. Each funder has questions specific to their requirements. The set of questions is also designed to screen out ineligible applicants. The online system will provide prompts to guide you through the questions to determine eligibility.

2.   Typeable Online Application Forms

Some funders use application forms in .doc, .pdf or other formats that have been designed with data fields that allow the applicant to type responses to questions.

- For some applications in .pdf format, information can be typed into the data fields, but once the forms are saved, it may not be possible to return to the application at a later time for additional editing. This format will require the applicant to enter all of the information in a single session. In this instance, a word processing application like MS Word® should be used to prepare a template of the application. This will create a separate document with responses to each application question. When completed, the responses can be copied into the corresponding fields on the .pdf form. Additional instructions and tips on how to create an application template are provided on pages 71-73.

  There are also some typeable .pdf applications that will allow you to *Save & Return* to edit and complete the process at a later time.

- For applications in the .doc format, information can be typed into the data fields and saved for later editing. In rare instances, you may encounter a funder who requests an e-mail submission of the completed application as a .doc file, or they may require that it be sent as a .pdf.

- For applications in formats that have been customized for funders, information can be typed into the data fields and saved for later editing.

For all types of typeable online application forms, the funder's guidelines will determine the format and method for completing and submitting the application.

Common Features of Online Applications

All online application systems include guidelines and instructions. Some include standard forms that have to be downloaded and printed. The format and process for completing e-apps will vary for different funders. Some commonalities and differences pertaining to online applications are highlighted below:

1. Instructions on how to complete the application are provided.

2. Some online systems will allow you to print a blank copy of the application or a list of the application questions. It is imperative to have this information, as it contains the details regarding everything that you will need to compile in order to complete the application. Prior to going online to enter information into the application, you must become familiar with all of the questions. This will ensure you have opportunity to gather all of the pertinent information, thus allowing you to prepare the responses in advance, according to the instructions.

    For systems that don't provide a feature that will allow you to view or print a document with all of the application questions, see page 73 for instructions on how to create a template that contains all of the questions.

3. In most instances, you will be able to "cut & paste" responses (including paragraphs with program information) into the data fields provided on the application. Most online applications don't allow basic formatting features like tabs, columns or character formats like **bold**, *italics*, underline or superscript.

4. Each data field on the application usually has a maximum number of words or characters that can be entered. Information about the maximum word or character count is usually placed immediately following each question, or adjacent to the data field. Some e-apps provide an onscreen feature that indicates the total number of words or characters remaining for the respective field.

    - Some e-apps instructions provide information about character or word restrictions. Some will simply indicate that you have exceeded the maximum word/character count when you attempt to move on to complete the next question on the application. By preparing responses to questions using a software like MS Word®, you can use the *word count* and/or *character count* feature to determine if you are within the stated limit, then copy the information into the online application.

    - Some e-apps will respond with an indication of how many words/characters have been entered; others simply indicate that you have exceeded the maximum word/character count.

5.   You may be required to enter financial Information for your program into data fields, or it may be required as attachments. Some online applications provide numeric fields or forms that allow the information to be entered and calculated automatically. If this isn't the format, it will be necessary to prepare your budget using a spreadsheet application (i.e. MS Excel®). Simply create a worksheet using their budget line items and categories. It will be easy to "cut & paste" your information into their fields, and you'll have a tool to use to make any future changes to the budget as needed.

6.   Most online systems allow you to save, review and print the document before clicking the SUBMIT button. In rare instances, some systems that use a typeable .pdf format for the application may require all of the information to be entered, completed and submitted in one sitting. This format will not allow you to save the document for editing at a later time. Fortunately this is not the most commonly used format. Some systems use .pdf formats that provide you with the opportunity to save or edit the document at a later time. Thus, it is very important to use a word processing system to capture all of the application questions and your responses in a document that can be edited as needed. This makes it convenient to copy the responses into the online application.

7.   Online applications usually include instructions and onscreen prompts to guide you through the process. As you complete one section, you will be prompted or guided to the next section. Most will allow you to return to previous sections to make changes. As you come to the end of each screen, the most common choices include:

   "NEXT" – *moves you to the next section or page of the application*

   "SAVE" – *saves all information entered up to that point and allows you to return to the application at a later time to edit and/or complete the application. May also be called "**SAVE & REVIEW**"*

   "REVIEW" – *allows you to review the complete application, with all responses entered up to that point. May also be called "**SAVE & REVIEW**"*

   "PRINT" – *provides a print out of the application with all information entered up to that point, including all of the application questions and your responses*

   "SUBMIT" – *transmits the application to the funder, with no opportunity to make any further changes. After clicking "SUBMIT" an auto-reply message will appear on the screen to indicate your application has been successfully submitted. Also, an auto-confirmation is usually sent to the e-mail that was entered by the applicant during the registration or sign-in process.*

How to Create Your Application Template

Creating a master document that includes all of the application questions is the best way to lay the groundwork to prepare your proposal. This will provide you with a single document, a central hub to gather and develop your answers to each question and make it easy to edit. It will also serve as a convenient source document which will be used to "cut & paste" information into online applications and onto standard application forms.

Instructions on how to create a document with all of the application questions is provided below:

Step 1: Open a blank document using a word processing application (i.e. MS Word®) and save it with a file name to identify the funding source, program for which the request is being made, and a date of reference for the application (Example: Barton Foundation – Youth Literacy – *MO/YR*).

Step 2: Logon to the funder's website to access the application. If their online format allows you to highlight and copy questions, "cut & paste" each question into your master document. This will create a template of the application. Be sure to include information about maximum characters or word count and other pertinent details that may be provided for each question.

Note: If the application is a .pdf document that does not allow you to "cut & paste," you may need to retype each question to create a template of the full application. If you have software like Adobe Pro®, you may be able to "unlock" the .pdf document to copy the questions.

Step 3: Finally, you can use your application template to record your responses and prepare your final edits. *You can use the character/word count feature for any questions that indicate a maximum limit before cutting & pasting your response into the online application.* *

As you proceed with lessons to learn The Grantbuilder™ approach to reviewing grant applications, you will become familiar with questions that are common across the funding spectrum. The illustration on the following page provides an overview of the ten most common categories of questions found on grant applications.

———————————

*See page 71, item 4 for review of character or word count.

Illustration 3

The 10 Most Common Grant Proposal Information Categories

1. **Mission Statement** – provides a succinct answer to this question, "What is the purpose for the organization?"

2. **History of organization and/or project** – provides information on when and why the organization was established, the principal parties involved and a summary of the programs and services offered.

3. **Description of project/program** – provides a detailed or summary overview of the proposed program.

4. **Goals & Objectives** – define desired outcomes that can be measured.

5. **Needs Assessment** – identifies specific needs or concerns that your program will address.

6. **Target Population** – demographic profile and description of population to be served by the project/program.

7. **Evaluation** – describes how the progress, success and effectiveness of your program will be measured.

8. **Timeline/Workplan** – indicates the schedule for implementing the components of the program. *For government grants, this item is often called a Scope of Work (SOW).*

9. **Future Sustainability** – describes plan for maintaining the program beyond any funding that may be awarded by the potential funder.

10. **Project/Program Budget** – provides a list of resources needed to operate the program and may require a *budget justification** or *budget narrative** (See pages 144 -148).

Most Commonly Requested Attachments:
- Proof of 501(c)(3) tax-exempt status (copy of the *IRS Determination Letter*)
- List of Board of Directors
- Copy of annual budget for 501(c)(3) organization
- Copy of audited financial statements for most recent fiscal year**
- IRS Form 990 (Annual Return for Organization Exempt from Income Tax)

*Brief description of items on the budget prepared to accompany a grant application
**An annual audit of your agency's financial records by a Certified Public Accountant (CPA) is a basic requirement for most funders. This audit is not specific to the programs or services that may be funded by their grant, but it is an audit of the nonprofit's financial records and practices overall. This document may be referred to as the *annual audit, financial audit* or simply the *audit*. (Referred to as the "single audit" for federal funders)

Note: An "Executive Summary" may be required by some funders. It should provide an overview of the entire proposal and limited to one page unless other instructions are provided.

Reviewing the Application

The Grantbuilder™ system includes the **Grant Application Review Worksheet** to make it easy to capture and record the most pertinent information needed to lay the initial groundwork for the actual grant writing process. As you identify potential funding sources, this worksheet is a useful tool for all types of grant applications. It should be used to record details for applications after you have determined that your program meets the funder's basic eligibility requirements.

It is designed to guide you through an overview of a funder's application to determine if the grant source is appropriate for your proposed request. The top section of the worksheet is used to record information about the funding source. The remainder of the worksheet has two columns. The left side has a list of questions and corresponding spaces on the right to record a succinct response. Once completed, the worksheet will provide a detailed, easy-to-follow synopsis of the application.

In most instances, all of the information needed to complete this one-page (two-sided form) will be found on a funder's website (or in other printed information) used for their grants programs under headings like "How To Apply," "Grant Guidelines," etc. There may be a few additional application-related instructions in other sections of their website or guidelines, which you may discover later during the process of preparing a detailed outline to write your proposal.

Instructions:

1. First conduct a quick review of all questions on the **Grant Application Review Worksheet** (pages 76-77) to determine eligibility (questions 5, 7 and 8),

2. Next, locate the section(s) in the funder's grant guidelines that contain information on how to apply,

3. Fill-in the top of the form with the funder's information. You may not be able to locate contact information for all funders. For some, the online application system will be the only means of communicating with them. You may be able to locate contact information for their headquarters or corporate office through research. However, if their instructions state they do not wish to be contacted, respect their request,

4. Read each item in the left column and record information in the right column as appropriate. Since guidelines vary among funders, you may not have information to respond to every item on this worksheet. If you do not find information that relates to an item on the worksheet, simply leave that item blank or insert "N/A" or "no info available," and

5. Finally, use the sections lableled "Other" to record any items required by the funder that are not already listed on the worksheet. List items that will require any type of follow-up, or any information that may be important to include as you prepare the application, or any other special instructions related to submitting the application.

Use this worksheet as a tool to build your knowledge base and personal library of funding resources. Over time, some funders may change their funding priorities, eligibility criteria or other parameters. If you use this system, it will be easy to update their information using the worksheet that you prepared for the particular funder.

Grant Application Review Worksheet

Funder:	
Website:	**Primary Contact**
	Name:
Mailing Address:	**Title:**
	E-Mail:
	Phone:
Application Login Info:	

Description of application item	Notes
1. Application deadline(s)? Postmark date or delivery date? *Indicate time zone for online submissions*	
2. Board resolution required? *If yes, it will be necessary to get approval, with signature of Board President/Officer*	
3. Initial LOI? or Full Proposal?	
4. Online or hard copy?	
5. Funders' mission/objectives?	
6. Range/Amount of grant awards? *i.e. minimum, average, maximum; also indicate if funding amounts are related to the size and age of an agency*	
7. Funding categories/ initiatives? *Ongoing? Special focus?*	
8. Funding restrictions? *Geographic, activity- or time-specific*	
9. Funding cycle? Schedule for announcement of awards? Payment schedule?	
10. Collaboration preferred or required?	
11. Letter of Intent? *(indicate major points and key details required)* Maximum pages?* Required information? Required attachments? **Pertinent to hard copy applications*	

Description of application items	Notes
12. Proposal Review Schedule? *Any indication of when a board, committee or other party reviews applications?*	
13. Information on how the application questions or sections will be scored?	
14. Funding history? Previous grantees? Range of amounts awarded? *Refer to funder's 990 for details if needed*	
15. Formatting and mailing/submission instructions *Special instructions regarding font size, margins (hard copies) or file formats for attachments (i.e. .pdf or .docx)*	
16. Attachments Required: - Board information? (resumes, summary bios or curriculum vitae?) - Proof of 501(c)(3)? - 509(a) status? - Proof of state's nonprofit status? - Letters of support/MOU's?	
17. Information required on staff positions that will play a key role? (resumes and/or job descriptions)	
18. Other:	
19. Other:	
20. Other:	

Additional Notes:

Exercise 5 – Reviewing Grant Applications

Instructions: Complete at least two (2) **Grant Application Review Worksheets,** one for each funding source indicated below.

1.   Complete a review for one of the **corporate** or **foundation** funding sources from Exercise 3 (page 44) or another corporate grant application of your choice.

2.   Complete a review for one of the **government** funding sources from Exercise 4 (page 48) or another government source of your choice.

Note: Record N/A (non-applicable) on the form if no information is provided for a particular item. Use the sections marked *Other* to record additional items as needed.

Preparing An Outline To Complete a Grant Application

After you complete the Grant Application Review Worksheets for Exercise 5 above, you will be prepared to select a funding source appropriately matched to your program. Next, prepare a detailed list of everything needed to complete the grant application. Paying attention to details during this part of the process will ensure you have all the information needed to develop a proposal that is thorough and competitive.

If the funder provides an application checklist, add their items to your list to include in your application review process. It is also critical to verify that all of the questions and other items required by the funder are included in your completed proposal. Diligence and attentiveness in preparing and using this detailed outline and checklist method will provide you with that guarantee.

It is important to use a method that will help you highlight every item in the instructions that has to be addressed in the proposal. Remember, your application will be competing against others being submitted. It is imperative to include everything that the funder has requested. The application may also provide you with information regarding how the proposal will be scored, including how many points or how much weight is given to each question or section of the proposal.

The **Grant Proposal Development Worksheet** (also referred to as the **Application Checklist**) is introduced in the following section. This grant writing tool is designed to capture and organize everything that the funder requests into an easy-to-follow format. The worksheet is designed with columns to list, summarize and track the completion of each question or other information required by a funder.

A single question on a grant application may require multiple responses. Therefore it is important to address each and every part of a question to ensure that your proposal warrants the maximum consideration by the funding source. One sample question is provided in the box below. This single question requires a response to four distinct items. Read the question and see if you can identify the four items.

Sample application question: What target population does this project serve (ages, ethnicity and gender), and where will the program be located?

Answer: Item 1 – Age groups/age ranges
(infants, youth, adults, seniors?)

Item 2 – Identify ethnic group(s) to be served

Item 3 – Indicate whether program is for males, females or both

Item 4 – Program location(s)

You can use the **Grant Proposal Development Worksheet** to review and document every question on an application. Once completed, you will have a detailed checklist of every item of information that the funding source requires. This activity also provides you with a detailed "walk-thru" of the entire application. Working through an application with such scrutiny is also a great way to organize your thoughts and generate ideas about the best approach to answering the questions.

If you fail to provide a full response to each question or item requested, you risk the loss of points, or in the worst instance, your application could actually be considered "incomplete" and disqualified from any chance to be funded. It is a waste of time and effort to submit an incomplete application.

Due to the intensely competitive nature of grant making, it is important to provide a response to everything requested in the application to ensure that your proposal will be given serious consideration.

Once you have completed the **Grant Application Review Worksheet** (pages 76-77) and decide to proceed with the development of a proposal, you will be prepared to complete the **Grant Proposal Development Worksheet**. Introduced on the next page, this worksheet provides a convenient way to review and document every item required by the funder. You can also use it as a detailed checklist prior to submitting the proposal to ensure that every question/request has been fully addressed, including:

1) Providing <u>complete</u> answers to every question,

2) Including <u>all</u> attachments as required, and

3) Following <u>all</u> instructions for submission
   (i.e. formatting and packaging for hard copy applications; file names or file formats for online applications)

Familiarize yourself with the use of each of the four columns in the partial worksheet on the page 81. A brief explanation for the use of each column is provided immediately following the worksheet. The worksheet on the following page includes three sample questions from a grant application, along with responses to illustrate the process. These examples illustrate how to use the worksheet to prepare a detailed outline. Using this method will help guide the development of your proposal and ensure a full response to everything requested by a funder.

> *Tip: As you review each grant application, pay attention to, and familiarize yourself with ...*
>
> *... Language and terms used* - (i.e. "low income" vs. "disenfranchised; "Mid-West" vs. "Middle America"). It will be to your advantage to incorporate the funder's language into your narrative when appropriate.
>
> *... The funder's mission, values, objectives, etc.* - Take the opportunity to describe how your program is aligned with their "big picture" goals.
>
> *... Funding priorities or areas of focus* – Provide clarity about how your proposed program fits within one or more of their priorities. Highlight features about your agency and program that are directly related to their priorities.
>
> This information will be very helpful as you begin to develop the various narrative sections to complete your application.

An Overview of the Grant Proposal Development Worksheet

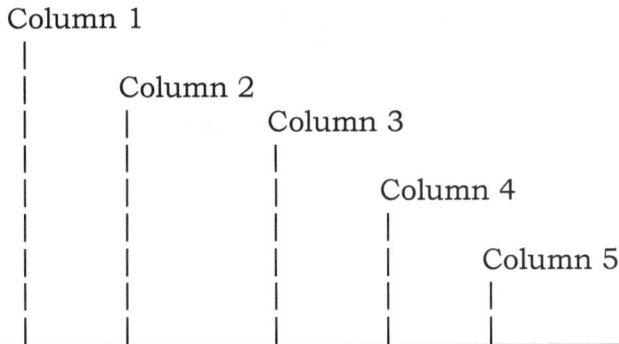

Column 1

Column 2

Column 3

Column 4

Column 5

Grant Proposal Development Worksheet				
√	Question or Item #	Add'tl Research Needed	Attach Add'tl Item(s)	Notes/Comments

Use of Worksheet Columns

Three sample application questions on the following page are entered onto the worksheet on page 84 to illustrate how this form is used.

Column 1 is used to create a **checklist "√"**, which will serve to verify that each question and item in Column 2 has been fully addressed and completed.

Column 2 is used to **record a number and/or letter combination that identifies each question**, each request for a document that must be retrieved or created, and other elements that will require a response.

Column 3 is used to list **items that will require additional research** to provide the information required (i.e. demographics of a particular region, high school graduation rates for a particular school district).

Column 4 is used to note additional documents (maps, resumes, newspaper articles, etc.) that must be submitted as **attachments** with the proposal.

Column 5 is used to provide a **succinct description of the items in Columns 1-3** and to record notes, additional instructions or other information needed to provide a full response to the corresponding question.

How to Use the Grant Proposal Development Worksheet
(aka "Application Checklist")

Three sample questions from a grant application are provided in the box below. Instructions on how to use the worksheet follow the questions below. Additional instructions are on page 84, along with an example of how to record these sample questions on the worksheet. An explanation of each entry is provided on page 85. A blank worksheet is provided on the next page.

Three Sample Questions

❑ Indicate the issues that this program will address and how you will measure the progress.

❑ Describe the target population, including the age group(s), ethnicity and unique characteristics.

❑ Identify the key individuals who will be involved in this project, along with their job titles. Provide a full resume for each person who will be working on the project for at least 20 hours weekly.

---

1. List each question on the worksheet using the procedure as illustrated in the example on page 84.

2. For each question, assign a specific number or alphabet to every single element contained within the question that requires a response. Each application question should be listed to ensure that you address each question in its entirety.

Tips:
- If the application already includes question numbers, you may use those to prepare your checklist.

- For multiple questions within one question, use a sequential alphabet or numbering system to identify each item that requires a separate response. *See examples on the sample worksheet on the following page.*

√	Question or Item #	Add'tl Research Needed	Attach Add'tl Item(s)	Notes/Comments

Recording Questions on Grant Proposal Development Worksheet

A brief description of how each column is used is provided on the worksheet below, followed by additional instructions. Each of the three sample questions from page 82 have been entered to demonstrate how to use the worksheet.

Column 1 - Check "√" to verify that everything for each numbered item has been completed before submitting the proposal

Column 2 - Record item # or question #; identify each element that requires a response

Column 3 - List items that require additional research to address

Column 4 - List items that require additional documents, attachments, etc. *(May already exist, need to be gathered or created)*

Column 5 – Brief description of what is needed

Tips: • You can cut & paste or type each question/item
• Use *italics* for notes that require follow-up

Grant Proposal Development Worksheet				
√	Question or Item #	Add'tl Research Needed	Attach Add'tl Item(s)	Notes/Comments
	1.			a. Issues/Problems addressed by this program b. How will you measure the progress?
	2.	( ) ( ) ( )		Describe... a. target population b. age groups *(current reports include this data)* c. ethnicity d. unique characteristics
	3.		( )	Gather copies of their resumes. List name and job titles of project staff.

Column 1 – Once you are able to place a checkmark next to each item, you will be assured that your application is completed. **Column 2** – Assign sequential pattern of numbers or alphabets to each question (I, II, III; 1, 2, 3; A, B, C). **Column 3** – Use blank checkboxes, parentheses or numbers that you can check-off to indicate that you have been able to identify the appropriate resources and followed up with the research needed to address the specific question. **Column 4** - The required items may already exist in files of the applicant organization or be available from some other source, may need to be gathered from other sources, or you may need to create them. **Column 5** – Include any details pertinent to answering the questions, specifically instructions to let you know what type of information to prepare or compile, where it might be located (file names, website links, professional colleagues to contact, etc.), or any other action that will be required to fully address the question.

Explanation of entries for questions on the previous page:

Question #1: Since this question doesn't require additional research or attachments, simply list each question (or item) in Column 3 that will require a response. Continue the process for each item on an application that will require an answer or response to satisfy the funder's requests.

Question #2: Specific data that involves research or the gathering of information is needed to respond to one or more parts of this question. Use the third column to create a checklist by placing a set of parentheses "( )" or a box "[ ]" in front of each item that will require a response. Each of these will serve as a reminder to follow-up to retrieve, compile or create the information or documents needed.

Question #3: Additional attachments are needed to respond to this question. Place a checkbox or set of parentheses "( )" in Column 3, followed by recording a concise description in Column 5 (Notes/Comments), of the item/paperwork that needs to be gathered. This may be an item that will require you to create a document.

Purpose for the Grant Proposal Development Worksheet

To create a content checklist to ensure that you have included <u>everything</u> required in the application instructions:

- *Assign an alphabet or number to every question or item that requires a response*

- *Review each of these items and make sure that you have done everything needed to check it off as completed*

Use A Numbering System to Create the Checklist

By assigning a unique identifying number to each item that requires a response, you will create a checklist that can be used to guarantee your proposal includes everything required per the funder's instructions. Alphabets are useful to identify multiple responses needed within one question. You can use the standard outline method to identify and record subsections of individual questions *(see **Three Sample Questions** example on page 84).*

Some funders use bullet-points to identify questions on their applications. However, you should use a numbering system to make it easier to reference and check-off the items as you work through the grant writing process.

If a funder uses a numbering system, you may choose to use theirs. However, you may still need to assign alphabets to identify multiple items within a single question. This will ensure that you track each item that requires a response (See sample questions 1 and 2 on the worksheet on page 84.

You can use boxes "☐" or parentheses "( )" to develop your checklist. This method will ensure that you can track whether you have provided a response to each question in its entirety. Later you will return to place a checkmark ☑ or an ☒ as you provide an answer or complete the requested item.

As you write the proposal, your completed **Grant Proposal Development Worksheet** will serve as your checklist to ensure that your grant application is completed as follows:

- Every question has been fully answered,

- Research to gather or create additional attachments has been completed, and

- The proposal is packaged and submitted according to the funder's instructions.

A blank copy of the **Grant Proposal Development Worksheet** is provided on page 83.

The **Grant Proposal Development Worksheet**

You can use this worksheet to conduct a thorough review of any application that you have selected to proceed with the preparation of a grant proposal. The layout of the worksheet facilitates a detailed overview of every item that needs to be addressed to ensure the preparation of a completed application. The worksheet will also help save time by providing a convenient summary of key points in one document. Proper use of this form will minimize the repeated flipping or scrolling back and forth through application instructions to locate or review detailed instructions as you write the proposal.

> **Tip:** If the funder that you select publishes an annual report, review it. This document provides additional information and insight into their organizational philosophy and the types of causes and projects of interest to them.

Once you have identified appropriate funding sources and reviewed their applications, it's decision time. Considering your schedule, do you have the time to prepare a complete proposal to meet the deadline? If the answer is yes, it's time to roll up your sleeves and delve into the grant writing process. Complete Exercise 6 to get started.

**Exercise 6 – Preparing the Grant Proposal Development Worksheet
(aka "Application Checklist")**

Instructions: Select one (1) of the applications from the completed assignment in Exercise 3 (page 44) or Exercise 4 (page 48). Use as many blank pages of the Grant Proposal Development Worksheet as needed to prepare a comprehensive checklist that includes each application item that will require a response. Be sure to document sufficient detail as follows:

1.   A brief description of each question (pay attention to requests for multiple responses within a single question),

2.   Items that will require additional research or other resources that require follow-up, and

3.   Additional attachments that must be submitted with the application (i.e. list of key staff, architectural drawings for capital project, map of community where service will be provided).

  a. Standard Attachments (i.e. IRS Letter, Agency Budget, Audited Financial Statements)

  b. Items specific to a funder's requirement or specific to a project (i.e. proof of liability insurance, medical license numbers for clinic staff, copy of vendor bids for equipment requested in a grant proposal)

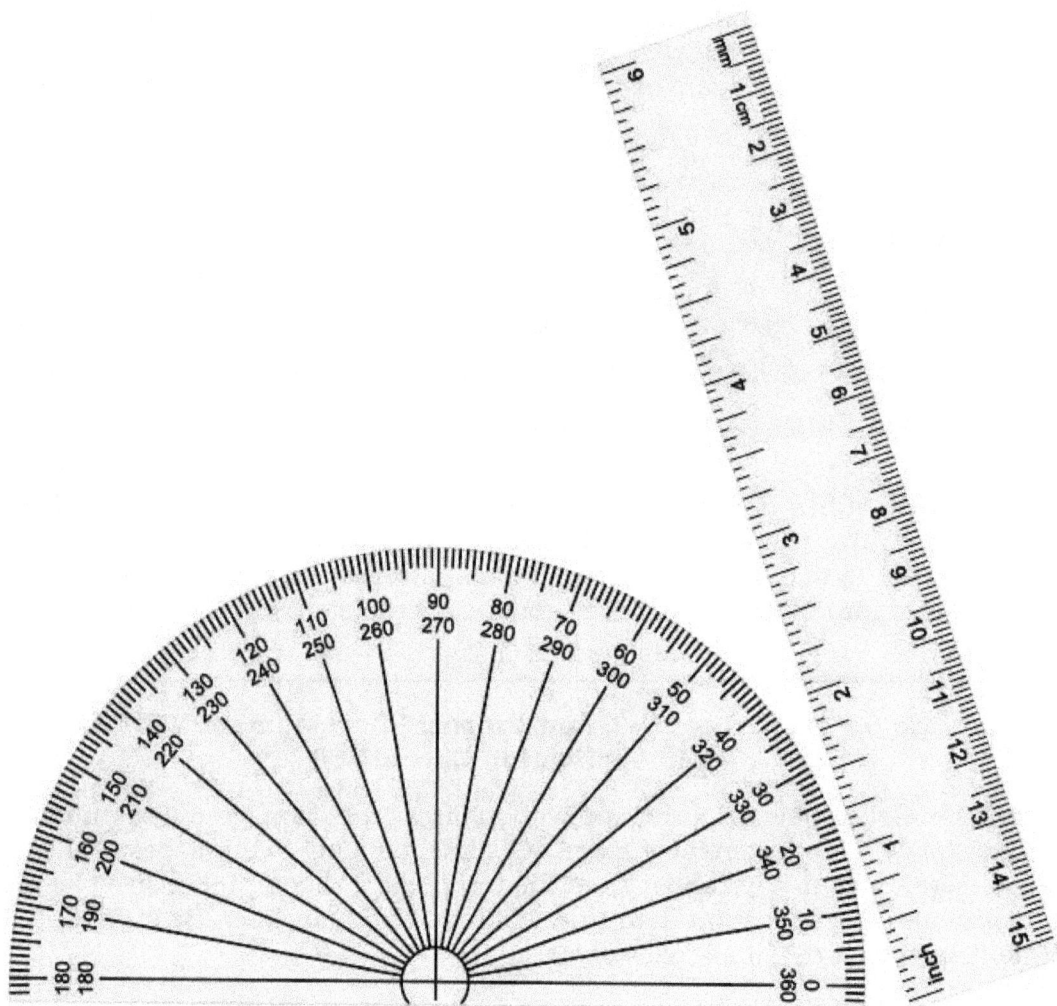

Part IV: Introduction to Program Design

This section provides a summary overview of the program design concept. The process is described and samples are provided as a guide to organize and package your ideas into a structure to make the grant writing process easier.

Upon the completion of Part IV, you will be able to create a program design that:

- Provides a clear and brief description of your idea or program

- Identifies the main activities and components needed to establish, implement, maintain or expand your program

- Prepares a summary budget for your program that provides a "ballpark" projection of the total cost for a twelve-month period (or other designated project period)

As you proceed with the completion of exercises in this workbook, concurrently it is important to begin the process of collecting and recording information onto the **Master Grant Data Worksheet** (Pages 180-231). If you will follow this recommendation, you will have all of the information needed to prepare any type of grant application by the time you complete this workbook.

Introduction to Program Design

Program Design refers to the process, as well as the structure that is used to create a project, program or service for implementation. The program design makes it easy to convey what the project is, how it will operate and the primary resources needed. The Grantbuilder™ system introduces a **program design outline**, which will serve as the framework for the development of a more detailed program description as you proceed through the grant writing process.

This workbook introduces a **Program Design Worksheet** as the first step to clearly define and describe the type of project, program or service that you wish to implement. It will provide the framework to expand on details to

> A fully-developed **program design** may also be referred to as a *service delivery model*, *program model* or *project model*

describe the various components of the program and how it will be implemented.

Once completed, the Program Design Worksheet provides a point of reference to help guide your grant research. This will save time by helping you focus on applications from funders that actually have a history of, or interest in, funding the type of program you propose.

Good program design begins with a thorough **needs assessment**, which is a fancy title to describe "why" a particular program or project is needed. You can use information you already have, readily available research or data gathered through other activities and resources. The Program Design Worksheet allows you to layout your concept in an outline format. It should also show a clear relationship to the needs assessment. Additional details will be added to describe the purpose and need for the program during the grant writing process.

The needs assessment may include research data gathered through formal and informal methods. The following is a partial list of resources and tools used to gather data for a needs assessment. It is important to incorporate information from sources, programs or individuals who represent the target population for your project. It is imperative to include data that reflects "third party validation" or opinions from recognized experts. All of this information will be used to inform the design of your program. You should use a combination of sources to demonstrate the need for your program, including:

- Feedback from clients, volunteers and staff (formal and informal, focus groups, written surveys, etc.),

- Existing data on client activities, progress, successes, challenges, etc.,

- Formal research (i.e. literature review of reports, articles and materials related to the type of program or service), and

- Media articles, reports and trends.

Be sure to design your program to include any special features required to address the needs of the population that you plan to serve.

- For example, if you are proposing a daytime career education program for single parents who have small children, you may need to consider childcare. Will your program provide childcare? Will you collaborate with a local childcare program? Will your program budget include client stipends for childcare? Will you simply prepare a list of local references to distribute to clients?

- If you plan to serve seniors who have limited mobility, it is necessary to plan for access and movement throughout the facility, as well as special accommodations if your program will include transportation. Will you have a wheelchair ramp at each entrance? Will you install handrails throughout the facility? Are your tables and desks at the proper height to accommodate wheelchairs and other seating that is higher-than-average to make it easier for constituents with mobility challenges?

Developing the *Program Design* also helps you to think about how the program will operate. Think of the Program Design as the first sketch of the complete floor plan to build a house – it provides an overview of the number and types of rooms, special features (fireplace, patios, etc.). Although it's only an outline, it provides a clear picture of what is planned and a general idea of the layout. Obviously, more detail will be needed to finalize the design, including an architect to add the features that will bring the initial sketch to life. It will also require the drawing of detailed blueprints to meet all applicable building codes. All of this takes place before the contractors can begin their work to bring the plans to life. Likewise, the Program Design worksheet creates the framework that will be expanded into a more detailed program description and budget as you prepare your grant application.

A good program design must communicate the project in a manner that is easy to understand and conveys the benefits to those who will be served. It increases the likelihood that a funder may take interest to help bring the design to life, or to support an existing program.

If you're not a strong writer, don't worry about correct spelling, grammar or sentence structure as you develop your *Program Design*. These skills are **not** critical to developing the concept and outline for the Program Design. The important thing is to formulate and structure your idea into a package that is easy to understand. Later, someone with a mastery of the written English language can proofread and edit the document.

Sample program designs are provided on pages 93-94. After reviewing the process and samples, complete Exercise 7 on page 94, using the worksheets on pages 95-97. These instructions and samples will guide you through the process, to place your vision or idea into an organized format that is easy to read and edit.

Five-Part Program Design Outline

The program design outline includes:

I.   The name of the project or program,

II.   A brief explanation of the program (should be no more than one paragraph),

       The description of your program design should highlight how it aligns with your mission, while addressing the goals and/or objectives of the funding source.

III.   An outline of the main service categories, activities and/or components of the program, and

IV.   A list of the staff, equipment, supplies and other resources required for the program.

V.   An estimate of how much money it will take to establish and operate the program for a minimum of twelve months.* This estimate is intended as a "ballpark" budget. The budget will be modified with specific details throughout the development of the grant proposal before it is finalized.

_____

*A 12-month period is used most commonly for grant funding cycles. In limited instances, you may need to use a shorter project period (i.e. for a time-limited, seasonal or summer project, a one-time week-long workshop series or conference, a multi-year project, or for a specific time period required by the funding source.)

Note: The Program Design Outline is an internal planning document used by the grant writer. It is not submitted with grant applications.

SAMPLE A
Program Design Outline

I. Proposed program: A Literacy Program for Disadvantaged Youth

II. Description: This literacy program will provide a series of 12-week workshops that consist of individual and small group tutoring using the "We Need To Read" program. The after-school and weekend program will recruit students, grades four (4) thru six (6) from communities in the Bay area.

III. Service Components:

Individual tutoring	"Spelling Bee" Contests
Small group tutoring	Certificates/Rewards for progress
Story writing contests	

IV. Resources Needed: (assumes that the space/facility is donated)

1 program coordinator (part-time) – certified teacher preferred	$10,000
3 tutors	6,000
"We Need To Read" program (2 sets & online learning modules)	800
Student notebooks, paper & writing materials (50 students)	300
Supplemental reading material (magazine subscriptions, books, etc.)	500
TV/Video monitor w/digital multimedia player	700
Digital/Audio player	300
Headphones for students	100
Chalkboard/Marker board (portable, stand with casters)	400
Office supplies	500
Total:	19,600
Administrative Overhead (10% of total):	1,960
V. Total Estimated Program Budget:	**$21,560**

Program Design Outline

I. Proposed program: A counseling and support services program for victims of domestic violence.

II. Description: This program will provide individual and group counseling, support groups and housing referrals for individuals and families with children in the Beatrick County area.

III. Service Components:

Individual counseling	Roommate referrals
Group counseling	Field trips
Crisis intervention	Batterer counseling referrals
Housing referrals	Childcare & children's activities

IV. Resources Needed: (1st 12 months)

Office space (2,000 square feet @ 1.00/sq. foot)	$24,000
Program Director	50,000
Counselors (3)	120,000
Childcare & Activities Coordinator	30,000
Furnishings & Equipment	5,000
Phone System & Service	3,600
Computer Network	4,000
Office Supplies	1,500
Multimedia equipment	1,500
Periodicals & Publications	2,000
Educational Materials & Supplies	3,000
Advertising & Outreach	3,600
Consultants	5,000
Estimated Budget:	$253,200
Administrative Overhead (10% of total):	25,320
V. Total Estimated Program Budget:	**$278,520**

The **Program Design Worksheet** on the following pages will help you outline the details for your project. Once you've completed your outline, you will have a better understanding of how and where all of the listed program components fit into the ten information categories required for most grant applications *(See page 74)*. It also provides a skeletal framework for the development of a brief LOI or summary proposal.

Exercise 7 – Developing Your Program Design

Instructions: Complete the three-page worksheet on the pages 95-97 for a project/program of your choice.

I.   **Proposed Program:** _____
       (Choose a title that describes the program or relates to the target population.)

II.   **Description:** *(Includes the following:* **What** *is the program?* **Who** *will be served, who will benefit?* **Where** *will services be provided?* **Why** *is this program needed?)*

_____

_____

_____

_____

_____

_____

III.   **Service Components:**

(List all the major categories of activities and events that involve program participants. What are the specific things that participants will do in the program? What are the major activities? – This section identifies the key resources that provide some indication as to **How** *the program will operate.)*

_____   _____

_____   _____

_____   _____

_____   _____

_____   _____

_____   _____

IV. Resources Needed (Part 1 of 2)
Program Design Worksheet - Personnel Budget
(Page 2 of 3)

List each part-time and full-time paid position needed to operate the program. Refer to page 132 for an explanation and overview of FTE's.)

Job Title	FTE	Monthly Salary	12-Month Budget
1.		$	$
2.		$	$
3.		$	$
4.		$	$
5.		$	$
6.		$	$
7.		$	$
8.		$	$
9.		$	$
10.		$	$
11.		$	$
12.		$	$
TOTAL STAFF WAGES:			$
ADD: BENEFITS @ 25%*:			$
TOTAL PROGRAM STAFF BUDGET:			$

*At the time of publication, this percent reflects the estimated amount for mandatory employer payroll taxes and other expenses typically related to employee compensation. Be sure to check national and regional data to approximate the current percent(s) and ranges for statutory employer payroll taxes, health insurance premiums and other obligations and benefits paid by the employer. The requirements and average rates paid for benefits will vary based on the state and region where the program will operate.

IV. Resources Needed (Part 2 of 2)
Program Design Worksheet - Operating Expenses
(Page 3 of 3)

Resources Needed: *Include <u>anything</u> and <u>everything</u> that will be needed to operate your program. It is useful to group related items in categories since most budget sheets included with applications tend to group expenses by category (i.e. personnel, facility, equipment, furniture, consultants)*

Line Item	12-Month Budget
	$
TOTAL OPERATING EXPENSES:	$
ADD: TOTAL PROGRAM STAFF BUDGET:	$
(from Page 2 of worksheet)	
PROGRAM STAFF AND OPERATING EXPENSES TOTAL:	$
ADD: ADMINISTRATIVE OVERHEAD (10%) OF TOTAL:*	$
V. TOTAL PROGRAM BUDGET:	$

Administrative Overhead (also referred to as *general operating expenses* or *operational costs*) - These expenses are needed to support the program and are not necessarily spelled out in a program's budget. Always include this line item in every program budget to account for incidental expenses associated with operating the program. This amount will contribute towards staff and resources that may have no direct involvement, however their roles in the organization contribute to supporting the program (i.e. occupancy/rent, insurance, receptionist, bookkeeping/accounting, management oversight, preparation of reports, janitorial services). *Ten percent of the total budget is the recommended rate to prepare the "ballpark" projection. See page 135 for additional information on Administrative Overhead.

Writing the Grant Proposal

Part V: Writing the Grant Proposal

This section provides instructions and worksheets used to gather and organize information needed to respond to grant applications. It also includes an overview of the process and resources needed to prepare responses to all questions on a grant application. Common guidelines for formatting and submitting completed proposals are also included.

Upon completion of Part V of this workbook, you should be able to:

- Review an LOI or grant proposal and identify the ten basic sections most commonly requested in funding applications

- Compile all information needed to prepare a complete grant proposal by using the following worksheets:

    - Program Design Worksheet (page 95-97)

    - Grant Application Review Worksheet (pages 76-77)

    - Grant Proposal Development Worksheet/Application Checklist (page 83)

    - Budget Development Worksheets (pages 138, 140-143)

    - Master Grant Data Worksheet (pages 182-231)

A sample grant proposal (including a cover letter, proposal narrative, budget, budget justification and timeline) is provided on pages 102-110. It addresses all major categories of information required by government, corporations and foundation funders.

As you proceed with the completion of exercises in this workbook, concurrently it is important to begin the process of collecting and recording information onto the **Master Grant Data Worksheet** (Pages 180-231). If you will follow this recommendation, you will have all of the information needed to prepare any type of grant application by the time you complete this workbook.

Basic Structure of a Grant Proposal

Unless specific guidelines are provided, most foundation proposals are usually two to five pages maximum. This does not include the budget or additional attachments that may be required. The 10 most common sections included in grant proposals described on page 74 are restated here. In addition to the four "Attachments" introduced on page 74, additional documents that are sometimes required, are indicated by a double asterisk (**).

- Mission Statement
- History of organization and/or program
- Description of project/program
- Goals & Objectives
- Needs Assessment
- Target Population
- Evaluation
- Timeline/Workplan ("Scope of Work" in government grants)
- Future Sustainability
- Project/Program Budget

Attachments

- Proof of 501(c)(3) status. This is the IRS *Determination Letter (aka IRS Ruling Letter)* and should always be included with your proposals, even if the written instructions do not request it.

- List of *board of directors*; sometimes requires a brief bio on each board member; may require a full resume for each director

- Financial information (items most commonly requested are indicated in **bold**)
  - **Annual agency budget for current year** (may require multiple years)
  - **Program budget** (if grant request is for a specific program)
  - **Copies of "audited" financial statement**(s) – usually requested for most recent one or two fiscal years. In limited instances, some funders may accept the most recent tax returns and/or financial statements prepared by a C.P.A. in lieu of a formal audit*
  - **Form 990** – Return of Organization Exempt from Income Tax (annual tax return required by the IRS for tax-exempt organizations)
  - *Copy of Business Liability Insurance***
  - *Copy of Workers' Compensation Insurance***
  - *An explanation of any unresolved audit findings***
- Board resolution (specific to government grants)**

Federal and state laws govern whether a nonprofit is required to undergo an annual independent audit based on the total amount and sources of revenue within the nonprofit's fiscal year. As of 2014, the federal government requires the audit for any organization that receives at least $500K in federal funds in one year. However, some states may require nonprofits to undergo an annual audit at a lower threshold and the amount will vary per state.

The following section includes a sample of a grant proposal for *Books 4 Boyz, a hypothetical* organization created for this example. It is prepared for a funding source that will consider maximum funding of $40,000 for this type of program. The proposal includes a program budget and line item justification. It does not include any of the attachments that would normally be required by a funder. It is prepared in a format appropriate for submission via hard copy or for online formats that may require attachments in .pdf format. All information in this sample would be appropriate to "cut & paste" into the appropriate data fields on an e-app, however some editing might be required to fit within "maximum" word or character counts stipulated by the funding's application instructions.

Exercise 8 – Identifying Basic Sections in Grant Proposals

Instructions: Identify the following elements as you review the sample proposal. Use the blank spaces to record brief descriptions or list key information for each item. Answers are provided on page 111.

- Mission Statement:

- History of organization or program:

- Program Description:

- Goals & Objectives:

- Needs Assessment:

- Target Population:

- Evaluation:

- Timeline/Workplan:

- Future Sustainability:

- Project/Program Budget:

SAMPLE
Cover Letter

(DATE)

Teresa Vanguard, Ph.D.
Chief Executive Officer
Youth Services Alliance Foundation
Anytown, MS 39090

SUBJECT: **REQUEST FOR FUNDING IN THE AMOUNT OF $40,000 TO EXPAND *BOOKS 4 BOYZ***

Dear Dr. Vanguard,

The *Books 4 Boyz* organization is requesting $40,000 from the Youth Services Alliance Foundation to expand a literacy program that has proven successful in improving academic performance and behavior for boys, grades 1-6 during the past year. Funding from your foundation will provide personnel, educational materials and related activities for additional children at the school to participate.

We look forward to hearing from you regarding this proposal. To learn more about us, please visit our website at www.34thStSchool.edu/B4B If you require additional information, please contact Principal Selina Trinski at (601) 987-6543 or strinski@34thstschool.edu.

Sincerely,

Selina Trinski, Ed.D.
School Principal
34th Street Elementary School

Enclosures: Grant application
                     Attachments
                     Books 4 Boyz Program brochure

34th Street School: Books 4 Boyz

Proposal for Funding to Youth Services Alliance Foundation

Mission Statement

Books 4 Boyz is established to encourage reading among school age boys, grades one thru six, to promote literacy and lifelong learning in communities where scores on standardized reading tests are below average.

History

Books 4 Boyz is a newly-established 501(c)(3) that began as a tutoring program for a group of boys who were having ongoing disciplinary problems at the 34th Street Elementary School in Cloverfield, CO during the spring of last year. When the principal reviewed the academic records and reading scores of 15 boys who were being sent to her office repeatedly, she became aware of a similarity among all of them – 60% of them had scored two to four grades below their appropriate reading levels. The remaining 40% were unable to read at the first grade level.

Two parent volunteers expressed interest in forming a structured program to tutor the boys in reading. Due to the lack of funds in the school's budget, the principal and four teachers began to hold car washes to raise funds for the "We Need To Read" program. Personal donations from teachers and other concerned parents at the school provided resources to send the two parent volunteers to the annual three-day, "We Need To Read" workshop during the fall of last year in Las Vegas, Nevada. Both completed the training and received certification as master trainers to conduct the program. They are authorized to train additional volunteer tutors, who are then eligible for certification.

The parent volunteers returned from the workshop and began to teach the program to 15 boys, grades 1 through 6, ages six thru 12. Twelve of the boys made the remarkable progress of advancing at least one grade level in reading after the first four weeks of the program. Each of the twelve boys benefited by having a parent or guardian take an active role in the home-study follow-up component of the program. The remaining three who did not have a parent or guardian involved made some progress, but not as significant as the other 12 students who had support at home.

In addition to an apparent increase in self-esteem reflected in improved behavior and cooperation from the boys with their primary teachers, the youngsters became involved in a number of the book reading contests at the local library. The competitive male instinct was reflected in their efforts to outdo each other as they openly shared and bragged to their peers about their newly-learned knowledge.

As knowledge of this successful program spread throughout the school, three things happened:

1)   All of the teachers at the school expressed an interest in having the program implemented as a regular part of the school's reading curriculum,

2)   The principal began to solicit donations and support from local businesses to expand the reading program to 100 students (20 girls and 80 boys) who had below-average reading scores and routine disciplinary problems, and

3)   Seven additional parent volunteers attended a two-day, twelve hour training conducted by the two certified instructors.

To date, 330 students have benefited from the "We Need To Read" program. The most recent test scores administered to the students indicate an overall average improvement of 3.5 grade levels for the current school year, the first full school year the program has been implemented.

Due to the slow, bureaucratic process of the public school district in supporting the expansion of the program, a motivated and dedicated group of parents and teachers sprang into action. After meeting with the principal and presenting the program at a school board meeting, the group raised money to have an attorney set-up a 501(c)(3), *Books 4 Boyz*. This provides the organizational structure needed to conduct fundraising activities, including the pursuit of grants. With organizational infrastructure now in place, they have committed time and resources to expanding this comprehensive literacy program to benefit the entire student body.

Proposed Program

Although the full-fledged program includes both reading and math components, the two-year implementation plan places a priority on the reading program for boys with disciplinary problems, accompanied by below-average reading scores. Hence, the *Books 4 Boyz* program.

Books 4 Boyz is designed to provide male children with a personal and school-based collection of traditional and internet reading materials of interest to them in conjunction with the "We Need To Read" literacy program. The book list is compiled from observing the categories and titles of books, magazines and websites most popular with boys who have participated in the program from its inception.

Funding is needed to provide the following resources for the successful implementation of this expanded program on a school-wide basis:

- Grade school reading materials (books and magazine subscriptions – hardcopy and online versions),
- Two computers for the school's library to provide access to online learning activities and internet reading sites,
- Twelve digital tablets to be rotated and shared among the classrooms for reading and related learning activities,

- Develop and maintain webpages and social media tools used to post and announce program activities and articles to acknowledge student achievement,
- Staffing includes one onsite program coordinator, one outreach specialist to facilitate the involvement of parents and guardians in the home-study component of the program, and three part-time assistants (tutors). The staffing plan provides consistency during regular school hours and ongoing training and support for the volunteers.

Books 4 Boyz is designed with two main components: 1) A comprehensive literacy enhancement program integrated into the standard curriculum during the regular school day, and 2) An after-school and/or weekend tutoring program that includes literacy research activities, book reading competitions and word recognition contests.

"We Need To Read" has proven effective in correcting deficiencies in reading scores for more than seven years. The program has been acknowledged as one of the top five reading programs for children in urban school districts. Developed more than a decade ago at the University of Wizby, it was initially tested in a pilot program at three elementary schools in Oakley, Philadelphia. At the time the pilot program began, the average reading scores at the three schools were at least 2.5 grade levels below the state average, which was one full grade level below the national average.

By incorporating reading material that is relevant to the curriculum in each classroom and of interest to the students, this program allows the instructors and tutors to customize the learning activities to fit the needs and interests of a particular student group. This aspect of the program has proven effective in encouraging children to migrate toward subjects that interest them and take an active role in their learning. This has resulted in an increase in voluntary reading activities by students in the program at the 34th Street Elementary School.

The program uses standard academic and social evaluation tools to determine areas of focus for each student. Pretests are administered to each student upon program enrollment and at the start of each major curriculum module in the *Books 4 Boyz* program. Post-tests are given to students after they complete each module to determine the rate and level of progress. Additional school records are reviewed and interviews are conducted with teachers and parents to determine overall improvements in behavior and academic performance.

Encouraged by these initial outcomes, the objective is to capitalize on the current momentum. Teachers and parents are eager to have this program as a mandatory complement to the school's existing reading curriculum. Routine record keeping will provide important information to assess the effectiveness of the *Books 4 Boyz* program in addressing literacy levels and behavior outcomes for boys at the school.

Books 4 Boyz will provide male children with an opportunity to master the skill of reading. As numerous studies have demonstrated, children who excel in school exemplify confidence and self-esteem. This has been proven again and again when academic excellence is the standard and expectation, even in the most challenging environments.

In a community riddled with violent crime primarily committed by adolescent and young adult males, these children need a helping hand. This program will give them lifelong skills and tools to rise above the statistics of high unemployment and a higher-than-average poverty rate per capita in their community. This program also plays a critical role in providing options for success by equipping male children with the gift of literacy.

Though this program is expected to address some of the special circumstances related to African American and Latino grade school boys, the "We Need To Read" component will benefit all children at the school.

Books 4 Boyz recently received notification of a $4,400 grant award from the Dipty Zap Foundation towards the purchase of digital tablets and computers needed for this program. A favorable response from your foundation for the full amount of $40,000 will provide more than half of the budget for a full school year. We have two additional grant proposals of $15,000 each pending with other funders. Additional proposals are being prepared for submission to a number of state-funded grant sources to support the program for a three-year period.

This program has already established a track record of fundraising success. In addition to a number of traditional parent-led fundraising activities that have involved the students (i.e. bake sales, car washes), the group has secured the services of a volunteer grantwriter who has agreed to prepare at least four grants over the next three months. The principal is also planning to include funds in the schools budget for the upcoming year to hire a part-time grantwriter

As the *Book 4 Boyz* leadership team comprised of parents and teachers becomes more knowledgeable about the board of directors' role in fundraising, a solid funding base will be put in place to support the organization. Fortunately, this program has a formal affiliation with the school, which provides readily available resources that don't require an expenditure of funds (i.e. facility for program activities; marketing and outreach using existing school communications with parents, students and teachers).

We are hopeful that the Youth Service Alliance Foundation will join others to contribute to the progress and success of this incredible program.

Program Budget Books 4 Boyz	
Personnel:	
Program Coordinator/Credentialed Teacher (.5 FTE)	$18,000
Instructional Aides	
(30 weeks x 7 aides x $10 hr x 4 hours)	8,400
Outreach Specialist (.5 FTE)	15,000
Total Wages & Salaries:	$41,400
Benefits (25%)	10,350
Total Personnel: A	**$51,750**
Educational Materials & Equipment	
Workbooks (300 students x $10 per book)	$3,000
Digital Tablets (12 x $200 each)	2,400
Internet Service & Data Plans for Tablets	1,200
Reading Program Tutorial Kits (3)	900
Website & Social Media	2,000
Digital Overhead Projectors (2)	700
TV/Video Monitors (2)	600
Equipment Stands on casters (2)	250
Portable Screen (1)	170
Portable Digital Stereo Equipment (2)	200
Computers (2)	2,000
Printing	2,000
Spelling Bee Event (2)	2,000
Magazine Subscriptions	1,200
Refreshments (30 weeks x $50)	1,500
Certificates (students & volunteers)	600
Postage	800
Total Educational Materials & Equipment: B	$21,720
Total A + B:	**$73,470**
Administrative Overhead (10%) of **Total:**	$7,347
Total Books 4 Boyz Budget:	**$80,817**

Budget Justification: Books 4 Boyz

Credentialed Teacher (.5 FTE) – coordinate program, train and supervise tutors and volunteers and function as senior tutor/instructor; prepare required reports. $1,500 per month x 12 mos. = $18,000

Instructional Aides – tutor and facilitate learning activities with students, volunteers and parents; provide training support to volunteers and parents. 30 weekends x 7 aides x $10 hr x 4 hours = $8,400

Benefits – statutory payroll taxes (social security, unemployment, workers' compensation and local payroll tax) estimated at 25% of budgeted salary = $10,350

Digital Tablets* – Twelve digital tablets to be shared among participating classrooms to support individual and small group learning activities. 12 x $200 each = $2,400

Internet Service and Data Plan – WiFi and internet access for computers and tablets used in the program. Discounted school rate: 12 mos. x $100 mos. = $1,200

Workbooks – educational materials for students. 300 students x $10 per book = $3,000

Reading Program Tutorial Kits – Three "We Need To Read" multimedia educational kits for program participants. 3 kits x $300 each = $900

Website and Social Media – design of Books 4 Boyz website to provide information and online enrollment and announcements for program activities. Design and distribution of information to promote and showcase program using popular social media tools. $1,500 one-time set-up and $500 for social media consultant to prepare and send announcements throughout the school year

Digital Overhead Projectors – equipment for transparencies used in multimedia learning kit. 2 x $350 each = $700

Portable TV Monitors – equipment used for multimedia learning activities on DVD included with the curriculum. 2 x $300 each = $600

Equipment Stands – portable stands on casters with locking storage compartment for multimedia equipment. 2 x $125 each = $250

Portable Screen – for learning activities that require the use of a computer/laptop and projector. 1 x $170 each = $170

Digital Stereo Equipment – MP3 players and iPod® for audio instructional materials. 2 x $100 each = $200

Computers* – desktops for placement in the library to operate multimedia software included in learning kit and inkjet printers; to be used for exercises and internet reading assignments recommended in learning kit. 2 stations x $1,000 each = $2,000

Printing – duplication of outreach materials, program handouts and orientation materials for staff and volunteers. $2,000 projected expenses

Spelling Bee Event – two school-wide events (one mid-year and one year-end) to recognize participants for their academic achievements; includes costs for refreshments, advertising, honorariums for celebrity host and bus tokens for low-income parents to attend.   2 events x $1,000 each = $2,000

Magazine Subscriptions – multiple copies of take-home reading material popular among target population (i.e. youth hip hop culture, car and sports periodicals). Also includes budget for several online and e-book publications. $1,200 projected expenses

Refreshments – lite snacks (fruit cups, juice, bottled water, cookies, paper goods, etc. for program participants). 30 weeks x $50 = $1,500

Certificates – design and production of Certificates of Achievement for students and Certificates of Appreciation for volunteers. $600 projected expenses for 300 students and 30 volunteers = less than $2 cost per participant.

Postage – Five mailings to approximately 250 households (student groups and volunteers). Approximately 400 pieces (first class postage) x five planned mailings, plus mailings of outreach materials to local educational programs. $800 projected expenses

Administrative Overhead – calculated at 10% of the total (A + B)

Funding has been secured for this line item.

* * *

Budget justification ends here

Some funders will indicate if they do **not** provide funds for administrative overhead. However, you still need to include this expense in your program budget. You'll simply have to find funds from other sources to cover this line item since it does represent an expense that you will incur to operate the program. Other funders may fund administrative overhead, but they will typically indicate the maximum allowed, usually as a percent of the total personnel or as a percent of the total budget. When they provide no indication, it is appropriate to apply a rate of at least 10% of the total budget.

A maximum rate of 12% to 15% applied to total Personnel (prior to the addition of Benefits) is commonly used for grants that emanate from a federal funding stream. An accounting professional with nonprofit expertise should be able to calculate a rate for administrative overhead based on your agency's annual operating budget.

	Books 4 Boyz Timeline/Workplan - Year 1
1st Quarter:	Develop and print outreach materials to inform parents of the program Purchase computer equipment and program supplies Recruit staff and volunteers for training Conduct first training for staff and volunteers Hire program coordinator and provide initial orientation to program staff and volunteers Commence program instruction Establish evaluation criteria
2nd Quarter	Conduct inservice for staff and volunteers Administer quarterly progress tests to students 1st Spelling Bee Competition Recruit and train parents to participate as classroom volunteers
3rd Quarter	Conduct inservice for parent volunteers Administer quarterly progress tests to students Develop outline for next year's program
4th Quarter	Conduct inservice for staff, volunteers & parents 2nd Spelling Bee Competition Administer quarterly progress tests to students Prepare year-end progress report Conduct year-end, post-test to determine progress Identify participants (students, parents & volunteers) for next year's program

Mission Statement – "Books 4 Boyz is established to encourage reading among school aged boys, grades one thru six, to promote literacy and lifelong learning in communities where scores on standardized reading tests are below average."

History of organization or program - this program began at the 34th Street School last year. It was inspired by a challenge with boys with repeated disciplinary problems.

Program Description - this is a school-based, literacy program that includes reading activities (hard copy and computer-based), contests and other interactive activities.

Goals & Objectives – to help students master and improve literacy skills, and improve behavior

Needs Assessment – behavior problems interfere with a student's ability to learn and contribute to low academic achievement and the ability to be successful later in life

Target Population – boys at the school, grades one through six

Evaluation – standard academic and social evaluation tools will be used (i.e. progress reports, report cards and standardized test scores); decrease in disciplinary incidents

Timeline/Workplan – the program will be fully implemented over a full year as indicated in the timeline on page 110.

Future Sustainability – the program has already received a $4,400 grant for computer equipment and additional proposals will be prepared to secure funding for a three-year period.

Project/Program Budget – total program budget is $80,817
(Personnel Total is $51,750)

Ready, Checklist, Write!

Getting Organized

Now that you have reviewed a complete proposal, you are ready to lay the final groundwork to write a grant proposal.

Getting organized from the beginning of the process will make your job a lot easier. It will be helpful to set-up a digital filing system with folders to facilitate easy access and retrieval of your information. Many grantwriters use a hardcopy system as a complement, including a set of folders for individual funders or grants, three-ring binders or organizing tools with the following sections, per grant:

Application & Instructions

Worksheets
(documents you will use, create or update as you develop the proposal)

Budget

Proposal (include hardcopy and computer file – disk, CD, etc.)

Supplements/Attachments

Follow-up (record of all correspondence/contact with funding source)

Miscellaneous Notes

Checklist to Start Writing

The following checklist of questions will help determine if you have covered all of the important preliminary steps for a specific application. This will make the proposal writing process much easier. (Page numbers are provided for convenient reference of documents needed)

Have you...

    ☑   ...selected the most appropriate funding application(s)?

    ☑   ...completed the *Grant Application Review Worksheet*? (76-77)

    ☑   ...reviewed all readily available information regarding the funder's grantmaking program?

    ☑   ...reviewed an annual report or other funder-generated documents that provide information about funding priorities? *(commonly available from foundation or corporate funders)*

    ☑   ...completed the three-page *Program Design Worksheet*? (95-97)

    ☑   ...completed the *Master Grant Template Worksheets*? (182-231)

    ☑   ...prepared the *Budget Worksheets*? (138, 140-143)

    ☑   ...given yourself enough time to complete the proposal to meet the deadline?

Be sure to complete each of these steps if you are serious about preparing a grant proposal that is both, professional and competitive. If you have answered yes to each of these questions, you're ready to move onto the next step. Going through the entire process will also lay the foundation to develop a master document/template that can be adapted to prepare multiple applications for your program(s). It is to your advantage to use everything at your disposal to maximize your chances for success in securing grants.

Common Guidelines for Formatting & Packaging

E-applications and online Applications that use pre-formatted data fields are designed with defaults and prompts to guide you through the steps needed to enter your responses to all of the funder's application questions. Some systems will indicate a limit for maximum words and/or characters allowed. If you exceed the maximum, some applications will prevent you from continuing onto the next question. Others state a maximum, yet their system may allow you to exceed the limit. However, you could be penalized with a reduced score on your application for failing to following the instructions. In a worst case scenario, your application could be disqualified. The solution is simple – **always** follow their written guidelines.

The guidelines noted in the following table apply to hard copy proposals, as well as some online applications that have to be prepared as text (or .pdf) documents and e-mailed to the funder.

Formatting Guidelines

Table 10

Basic Rule	Purpose
All information is typed	Easy to read
Maximum pages	The funder either wants the applicant to condense the information onto a limited number of pages or to elaborate in a lengthier proposal
Pages/Sections required to be placed in a certain order	It makes it easier for grant reviewers to review numerous grant proposals when all applicants adhere to a standard of uniformity
A certain number of copies of the proposal are required	Provides a copy for each member of the grant review committee
There is often a minimum font-size requirement	To make it large enough to be legible and to discourage applicants from "stretching" beyond the maximum page length by using a smaller font
There is sometimes a requirement for the document to be single-spaced or double-spaced	Funder preference for their own purposes (i.e. single space saves paper, double-spaced allows room to write notes during their review)
There is often a minimum margin requirement	To discourage applicants from "stretching" beyond the maximum page length by reducing the margin size
There are usually specific instructions regarding binding	Makes it easier for the committee to flip through and compare information on different pages during the review process

114

Formatting Tips

For proposals that don't require the use of standard application forms or online systems, it is acceptable to present information in the order listed in the application. The only exception is when doing so would make the respective section of the proposal awkward and difficult to read.

Use **<u>Headings</u>** to identify each major section of the proposal, in the order they are presented in the funder's application (or guidelines). This applies to hard copy proposals, as well as narrative sections prepared for a proposal that will be submitted online as an attachment. This does not apply to e-apps that provide separate data fields.

Always follow the funder's formatting guidelines. Six of the most common to consider for hard copy proposals are listed in the left column of the following table. These guidelines also apply to hardcopy and downloadable formats that have to be printed and submitted via e-mail or mail delivery. If no guidelines are provided, it is acceptable to apply the formatting guidelines noted in the right column.

Formatting Item for Grant Proposals	Acceptable Standard *Commonly used in absence of specific guidelines*
Font size and style	Times Roman or Arial, minimum 11-12 pt font
Margins	One-inch
Line-spacing *(single, double?)*	Narrative, single-spaced; single or double-spaced to separate paragraphs
Number of copies *(one-sided, two-sided?)*	One-sided makes it easier to replicate; does not apply to attachments that may already be formatted as double-sided documents (i.e. financial audit, 990 Form)
Maximum page length *(per section and per proposal)*	Three to five pages maximum, not including attachments
Binding *(staples, paper clips, rubberbands, "Do Not Bind," etc.)*	Paper clip or staple the proposal narrative, along with the program budget. It is common to include one or more standard, multi-page attachments that may be stapled as complete document sets (i.e. Board List, Agency Budget, Financial Audit, 990, etc.)

Preparing Your Application Template for Grant Writing

It is imperative to prepare a master application template. Tips to prepare templates from hardcopy applications and ".pdf" document formats are summarized below. Instructions for working with e-apps are provided on pages 67 and 69-73.

Hard copy applications

- If the funder provides a typeable hardcopy document, simply save a copy and use it as your master application template for the specific grant proposal.

- Make at least one extra copy of the set of application forms provided by the funding source. In the event you make a mistake while printing information on a hard copy, you will have a clean copy to print the final version of your application.

- Some application forms can be downloaded and printed. Others may have to be scanned or saved for conversion into a PhotoShop® file, .pdf or other format that can be set up to accommodate typing.

- Some grantwriters find that having a hard copy of the application is useful for taking notes, which can serve as an aide to guide the writing process.

- Keep the application pages in order. A folder or three-ring binder is useful for this purpose. As simple as this may sound, it will save you valuable time if you need to refer to the application to review any detailed instructions.

> *Always prepare a master application template that contains all questions from the e-application (e-app) or online application*

It is important to save a blank copy of the master template. You should make a separate copy to prepare the proposal narrative. Blank applications are very useful for comparison when re-applying to the same funder at a later date. If there are no significant changes to the application form or questions, you may be able to revise and update sections of information from the prior application submitted. Using responses from an existing grant proposal as a starting point will save a significant amount of time, expedite your grant writing process and help you get more applications into the hands of funders for consideration.

Tips for Online ".pdf" Document Format

For online applications created using a ".pdf" format, use an application like Adobe Professional® to convert it into a format that will allow you to edit the information. If you don't have software to make the conversion, it will be necessary to download and print a copy of the application, then type each of the questions into a document to create the master application template. (See page 73 for instructions)

Illustration 4

Laying the Groundwork for E-apps

The following steps may be used for e-apps that have to be completed and submitted online in their entirety.

Step 1:   Logon to the funder's website (or link that is provided) to access the application questions. You will likely be required to complete an eligibility quiz to gain access to the questions (see page 69).

Step 2:*   Prepare the **Grant Proposal Development Worksheet** (see page 83) to use as your primary source document. Cut and paste each of the questions into a wordprocessing document to create an application template. This will make it easy to develop and edit the proposal. Check to determine if a maximum word or character count is provided for each field, and be sure to note this detail beside each question/item as well. This information will serve as a guide to help you prepare responses in appropriate lengths.

Step 3:   Save a copy to develop your master application template.

Step 4:   Prepare and type responses directly into the template for each of the questions.

Step 5:   Review and edit your master document as needed to create the final version.

Step 6:   Cut and paste the responses to each question into the data fields in the online application.

Step 7:   If applicable, complete the process to include each of the required attachments.

Step 8:   If the option is provided, follow the instructions to print a copy of the completed proposal before clicking on the "SUBMIT" button. Review the printout to determine if any additional edits are needed.

Step 9:   Once you have verified that the entire application is accurate and complete, press "SUBMIT." Always save, print and file both a digital and hardcopy of your completed application, including any auto-reply confirmation notices from the funder related to the submission of your proposal.

Developing the Proposal

As you write the sections of your proposal, be mindful of the funder's priorities, goals and language. Use this information to inform the tone and content for your proposal. Is the tone academic? Do they use terms common to a certain professional discipline? Be sure to incorporate some of their language and tone throughout your proposal as appropriate. It is a fine balance between an art and a science to accomplish this feat without appearing redundant.

As You Write...

One of the most important things to remember when responding to questions or items on the application is...**be sure to provide a complete response to each question or item on the application.**

Your response should clearly answer the item or question <u>before</u> you espouse your philosophy, experiences or examples. With anything less than a full and direct response, you run the risk of not answering the question fully. It is easy to go off on a tangent with excitement about your project. But remember, you are presenting your idea to someone who may not have background or knowledge about your organization, geographic area, or the type of program that you're proposing.

Questions on an application are designed to provide the funder with information they need to make an informed decision. It is better to give a one or two sentence answer that fully addresses the question rather than writing a paragraph that doesn't get to the point.

Individuals who participate on grant review committees typically have experience writing proposals or operating programs funded by grants. They will likely be able to distinguish between a fully-developed answer and a superfluous response padded with unnecessary words, explanations and examples.

Grant review committees are impressed with proposals that demonstrate attention to detail, starting with adherence to the instructions. This sets the stage for a very favorable "first impression" as they review your completed application. There is favorable perception and sometimes an assumption that an agency (or individual) attentive to the guidelines and details involved in preparing a proposal, is likely to apply the same standard to running the proposed program if a grant is awarded.

It will required extensive preparation, writing and proofreading on your part to have your proposal viewed in a favorable light, but it will result in a highly professional proposal that is impressive and competitive.

Writing Tips: Developing the Proposal Narrative

Use your **Grant Proposal Development Worksheet** to record all of your responses and edits. As you commence the writing process, continue to take notes as ideas arise. It will be helpful to create an additional "notes" file or add an extra page to the bottom of your template for this purpose. Later, when you get to sections that relate to specific notes, you can "cut & paste" the note into the appropriate section for further development, editing and/or follow-up. It is helpful to identify your notes by applying a different format to the font to distinguish them from your proposal narrative (i.e. color font, italics, bold).

Review your checklist to identify any relevant writing guides that need to be considered. You can continue to add notes to the template to inform your responses for specific sections or questions. Copy & paste the notes as needed, which will be deleted when you prepare your final draft.

Consider everything in your program narrative that will require a payment or purchase. This includes any resource that will be needed for the program to operate. If you include a description of anything in the narrative that is not already included in the draft of your budget, record it on the "Notes" page. You will use it later to finalize the budget for the respective program or grant.

As you write, show a relationship between the funder's philosophy and your program. Incorporate the funder's language and wording throughout your proposal. Pay attention to phrases and terms that funders use to refer to the target population, funding priorities and other items that can help you shape your narrative to align with their language.

Whenever possible, provide a one sentence response that is complete and easy to understand for each question. Even if you expand on the sentence with further explanations or examples, it is important to first provide a direct and complete answer to the question. Respond with an answer that addresses each question in its entirety. Use simple words whenever possible.

Integrate information from evidence-based research studies (formal & informal) to demonstrate your understanding of the type of program that you are proposing. If space allows, include the reference or citation for the research in the body of the narrative (or as a footnote in hard copy proposals that may provide additional space).

Use graphs, charts and tables to convey useful information. These visual elements can be included with hard copy applications. You can also place them within documents for online applications that allow extra attachments in addition to the budget, IRS letter, board list and other documents most commonly required. Currently, most online systems are designed with data fields to accept only basic characters, numerals and symbols. Formatting options are usually limited to the use of CAPITALIZATION, and sometimes the **bold** and <u>underline</u> features.

Final Review and Proofreading

After you prepare a draft of the entire proposal, have one or more individuals review the document. Ask them to read it and provide feedback. Use their feedback to determine where you might need to clarify certain information.

Review each section of your proposal, word-by-word. Use your **Grant Proposal Development Worksheet** as your final checklist to ensure that each and every item has been addressed.

If you're not 100% confident about your writing skills, have someone with a mastery of written English proofread and assist you with editing your proposal after you have prepared your initial draft.

Even if you have 100% confidence in your writing skills, it is important to have another person with a mastery of written English skills review your proposal. They don't have to be familiar with the topic. In fact, if they understand the program described in your proposal after reading it, you will be assured that you have explained it well.

The purpose for their review is to provide feedback that may be used to edit and improve the proposal. Specifically, their input will:

1) Serve as an indicator of whether you have communicated what you intended, and

2) Identify typos, other errors or inconsistencies in the proposal

Ready To Write?

Congratulations! By following the step-by-step process in the prior sections of this workbook, you are prepared with the knowledge and skills to prepare a complete grant proposal. Use the checklist below to determine if you have laid the foundation necessary to proceed. Complete all workbook exercises associated with the five items on the list below, then move on to Exercise 9 on page 121.

- ☑ Program Design (pages 95-97)
- ☑ Grant Research *to select the funding source* (pages 41-46)
- ☑ Complete Grant Application Review Worksheet (pages 76-77)
- ☑ Prepare Grant Proposal Development Worksheet (pages 83)
- ☑ Create Master Grant Data Worksheet (pages 182-231)

It is important for you to complete the exercises and worksheets related to items on the checklist **before** proceeding with the grant writing process. By completing the five items listed above, you will have the foundation needed to prepare a professional proposal that can be submitted and considered for funding.

Developing Your Proposal Narrative
Exercises 9, 10 & 11

These exercises provide hands-on grant writing experience as you prepare all of the narrative sections required by a funder. First, make a decision about the specific organization or program for which you will prepare a proposal. Second, record information for your organization and program into all applicable sections of the **Master Grant Data Worksheet**. *It is imperative to have this multipage worksheet completed at this point, as it will allow you to "cut & paste" information to respond to all of the application questions.* Finally, use your completed documents from the three following workbook exercises <u>or</u> prepare a new set to proceed with completing a proposal for your program.

- **Program Design Worksheet** (page 95-97)

- **Application Review Worksheet** (pages 76-77)

- **Grant Proposal Development Worksheet**/Application Checklist (page 83)

After you complete Exercises 9 and 10 below, the budget and timeline will be the only remaining items needed. The next two sections of the workbook provide an overview, instructions, samples and worksheets to guide you through the development of budgets and timelines required by funders.

Exercise 9 – Create Your Grant Application Template

Instructions: Create a master grant application template that includes all questions and items from the funder's application. *In addition to serving as your writing guide, this completed document will also serve as your checklist to ensure that all of the items required by the funder have been addressed.*

Exercise 10 – Develop an Initial Draft of the Proposal Narrative

Instructions: Using information from appropriate sections of the **Master Grant Data Worksheet** (pages 182-231), enter a response to each question or item on the master grant application template from Exercise 9. At this stage, the priority is to provide a response to each item. *You will edit the responses during the editing process to adhere to the funder's instructions* regarding the maximum character or word count.

Be sure to check-off each item that has been completed. *It is understandable that your responses may not be fully developed yet, however, you will have opportunity to make additional edits after you have entered information in response to each question. If you have followed instructions to work on the **Master Grant Data Worksheet** as you have proceeded through this workbook, you will be able to "cut & paste" information from sections that have data relevant to the specific application question(s).*

Common Formatting and Submission Guidelines

The most common formatting and packaging requirements are described below. *The items in* **bold** *text apply to hard copy formats only.*

1. Font – the majority of online (e-apps) have a default font, which the system will automatically apply to any information that you "cut & paste". For formats where the completed application will be submitted in hardcopy, the funder may require a specific style and/or maximum size to provide consistency across all submitted proposals to make it easier for the reviewers. For some online typeable .pdf applications, the funder may request a specific font to ensure that your proposal will retain the correct format when they open and download the document on their end. Among the most commonly requested fonts are Times New Roman and Arial.

2. **Number of copies** - if multiple copies are requested, it is usually an indication of the number of individuals on the grant review panel for the proposals.

3. **Special mailing instructions** – may entail a request for delivery by USPO, by overnight carrier or certified mail, which will verify the date the proposal was mailed. Remember, pay attention to "postmark" versus "due in our office by (date/time)" deadlines.

4. **Wet signature** – may request a "wet" (original) signature in blue or black ink by an authorized party

5. **Special binding/packaging** - makes it user-friendly for the funder to process, file and retrieve grant application documents within their filing system (i.e. no staples, required use of a rubber band or paperclips to bind each set of copies, place in a 3-ring binder); if they request only one copy, do **not** place the pages of your proposal inside of individual, plastic sheet protectors or a portfolio-style folder with binding. It will make it cumbersome for the funder to dismantle the individual pages if they need to make copies for members of a grant review committee.

6. File names and file formats – some funders may request a specific format to assign file names to application documents, including attachments. This creates a standard name format to make it easy for the funder to identify documents from numerous applicants. File types like .docx, .pdf, etc. may be required.

Exercise 12 – Preparing for the Formatting Requirements

Instructions: Select one of the applications that you reviewed in the previous exercises and record the basic formatting guidelines on the lines below:
(if no specific instructions are provided for any of the items below, mark *N/A)*

Indicate type of application: (   ) hard copy   (   ) online

Formatting/Packaging Item	Funder's Requirement
1. Margins*	
2. Line-spacing*	
3. Number of copies*	
4. Number & names/types of attachments	
5. Special binding/mailing instructions*	
6. File name formats (for online submissions, if applicable)	
7. Other	

Applies to applications prepared to submit in hardcopy (or .pdf format created by the applicant that required a copy to be emailed or mailed)

Part VI: Budget Development

This section provides an overview and instructions on the basics of developing budgets that must be submitted with grant applications. It includes both annual and program budgets.

After completion of this section, you should be able to:

- Know the difference and relationship between an annual budget for an agency, in comparison to the budget for a specific program or project

- Understand the basic structure of a budget

- Develop a detailed program budget and *line item budget justification* with appropriate expenses for staff, administration and program activities

- Understand the meaning and use of *full-time equivalents (FTE)* to calculate salaries and wages for personnel

- Demonstrate a basic understanding of how Administrative Overhead or Indirect Expenses impact budget development and the importance of including this item

As you proceed with the completion of exercises in this workbook, concurrently it is important to begin the process of collecting and recording information onto the **Master Grant Data Worksheet** (Pages 180-231). If you will follow this recommendation, you will have all of the information needed to prepare any type of grant application by the time you complete this workbook.

The Agency's Annual Budget

Funders usually request a copy of the applicant agency's annual budget, as well as financial statements. They may provide a budget form. In the event that no specific instructions or standard forms are provided, a copy of the annual budget for the current fiscal year should be submitted. Annual budgets may be prepared in a variety of formats and lengths. Any organization that currently provides programs and services should have an existing annual budget. This financial document may range from a one-page version that summarizes all major categories and amounts, or it may be a multiple page document that includes more details.

Is your grant request for a specific program? ...

... If so, you will need to prepare and submit a separate program budget as well.

Some funders may also request a copy of an operating statement and balance sheet for the most recently completed fiscal year, or other specific time period. Their written guidelines will indicate all of the financial records required.

If you are requesting funds for general operating expenses (as opposed to a specific program), a copy of your agency's current annual budget will be required along with the application. If an annual budget does not exist, a projected twelve-month budget should be prepared to reflect all expenses associated with running the agency. The budget should list all sources of anticipated support, including other grants, cash donations and *inkind* goods and services. (See page 134 for an explanation of *inkind* donations.)

The example on the following page is a condensed version of an annual budget for a nonprofit organization with a relatively small budget. It presents a scenario of how each line item in an annual budget might be covered by a combination of resources. Footnotes at the bottom of the page are provided to explain information listed in each of the columns (i.e. Personnel, Facility).

Is your grant request for a newly-established nonprofit? ...

... If so, "inkind" and cash contributions are often the major categories of support included in the annual budget.

(Agency Name)
(Year) Annual Budget

	Total Budget	Grants[1]	Inkind[2]	General Fund[3]
Personnel	$130,000	$80,000	$20,000	$30,000
Facility	17,000	8,000	-	8,000
Furniture	5,000	-	5,000	-
Computer Equipment	3,000	-	3,000	-
Conferences/Training	3,000	-	-	3,000
Office Supplies	1,000	-	-	1,000
Utilities	2,000	-	-	2,000
Insurance	1,000	-	-	1,000
Total Budget:	**$162,000**	**$88,000**	**$28,000**	**$45,000**

[1]The "Grants" column includes funds that have been obtained through the grant application process.

[2]The "Inkind" column includes donations of non-cash resources, tangible items and services that can be assigned a dollar value. The amount should reflect a reasonable amount or current market value the organization would have paid for the budget item, if the resource had not been donated.

[3]This "General Fund" column includes items covered by cash from all other sources, including fundraising activities, cash donations and reimbursable out-of-pocket expenses by persons involved with the organization.

See the following page for another example of a one-page budget for a different organization, Central Youth Center, Inc. This annual organizational budget is prepared in a simple, two-part format (revenue and expenses).

An annual budget may include line items that represent summary calculations of multiple line items *(i.e. the total for a Salaries and Wages line item represents the total of all expenses in this category for numerous employees)*. The following budget includes items that have been calculated from the agency's accounting records or worksheets to derive each item and amount listed. The pages that follow will walk you through the process needed to develop detailed summary budgets similar to this format.

Central Youth Center, Inc.
(Indicate Year) Annual Budget

REVENUE

Grants	403,000.00
Individual Donations	45,500.00
Fee-for-Service Contracts	689,000.00
Special Events	203,000.00
Holiday Donation Campaign	41,600.00
TOTAL REVENUE:	1,382,100.00

EXPENSES

Salaries & Wages	748,000.00
Payroll Expenses	172,040.00
Accounting & Annual Audit	23,000.00
Advertising & Marketing	16,200.00
Community Outreach	15,000.00
Computer Equipment & Software	16,500.00
Consultants	103,000.00
Facility Rent & Maintenance	85,000.00
Fundraising	132,000.00
Insurance	9,300.00
Memberships and Subscriptions	5,600.00
Mileage Reimbursement	6,800.00
Printing & Postage	24,370.00
Professional Development	12,000.00
Office Supplies	8,290.00
Social Media	5,000.00
TOTAL EXPENSES	1,382,100.00

The Program Budget

The program budget should include everything needed to support the proposed program. Expenses should be reasonable for the type of program, staff and other resources required for its operation.

Some grant applications include a standard budget form (or set of forms). In the event that no standard forms are provided, budgets should be prepared according to generally accepting accounting principles. The budget should be prepared with spreadsheet software to minimize the chance of calculation errors. If needed, budget numbers can be transferred onto application forms later.

Each item listed on a budget is referred to as a "line item", hence the name "line item budget." All amounts should be rounded off to the nearest $10, $100, $1,000, etc. depending upon the size of your total budget.

This workbook introduces the development of a budget that has three main sections as noted below. Additional detail will be added to prepare the final budget that will be submitted with the proposal. Pages 131 and 134-136 include additional budget information regarding personnel, operating expenses and administrative overhead.

1) Personnel

Subsections may include: Employee salaries and wages, group health insurance and other employee benefits, as well as employer payroll taxes.

2) Operating Expenses

This section includes a list of major categories of all expenses required for the program to function. Related expenses should be grouped into categories. For example, all expenses related to information technology may be grouped under an "I.T." subsection, or all services to be provided by independent contractors may be listed under a "Consultants" subsection. Operating expenses may also be referred to as "Program Expenses" when the line items are for a specific program.

3) Administrative Overhead or Indirect Costs/Indirect Expenses

Each agency should select a method or formula to establish a rate (%) that will be applied to calculate the "unseen" costs for operating programs. There are different approaches, including but not limited to:

- Percent of personnel expenses
- Percent of total budget
- Allocation of square footage used by specific programs

Budget Structure

Unlike budgets prepared for "for-profit" businesses that begin with a *Revenue* section, budgets prepared to accompany a specific request for grant funds often have two major sections: personnel expenses and operating expenses. Additional subsections may be used, with numerous line items under each section. An example of a budget outline prepared in a standard accounting format for a nonprofit grant application is illustrated below.

Agency/Program Name	
(Year) Budget	
Personnel Expenses:	
Salaries & Wages	$
Employer Payroll Taxes	
& Employee Benefits	$_____
Total Personnel:	**$**
Operating Expenses:	
List by alphabet or group by similar category	$
	_____
Total Operating Expenses:	**$**
Administrative Overhead or Indirect Expenses:	$
	_____
Total Budget:	**$**

It is important to make detailed notes on how each line item in your budget was calculated. In addition to using the information to manage your program, you will find the information useful if a funder requests budget details in the future. If your program is funded at an amount lower than the initial request, which is usually the case, the original calculations will serve as a point of reference to make adjustments.

Many funding applications include one or more questions about the agency's revenue (i.e. Dollar amounts and/or percent of revenue from government grants, individual donations, sponsorships, investment income). The applicant may be required to enter the information onto a budget form or into data fields on an online application.

Note: This budget is not the same as the annual budgets, operating statements, balance sheets or other financial documents that the funder may also request as attachments.

Personnel include all full-time and part-time staff members who will operate or support the program. Every job position included in this section is for staff that receive payment of salaries or wages through the agency's payroll system. These individuals submit timecards or timesheets and receive a paycheck on a regular schedule. The agency is responsible for withholding and paying all applicable employee payroll deductions to federal and state entities on behalf of the employees. At the end of each calendar year, the employer is also responsible for preparing a W-2 (Wage and Tax Statement) with details of total amounts paid and taxes deducted for each employee.

Salary ranges can be obtained from a number of sources, including online resources, contacting a local nonprofit with similar positions, asking friends or associates who hold similar positions, logging onto the internet and typing "salary information for (JOB TITLE)" into your favorite search engine, and researching local classified advertisements for job listings that include salary amounts.

Additional amounts must be included to account for employer payroll taxes, health insurance premiums and other statutory personnel expenses. As of the writing of this workbook, this amount ranges from approximately 20% to 25% of the salary amount and should be included in your budget computations. Please check with a local bookkeeper or accountant who is familiar with current rates for standard payroll taxes in your area (social security-FICA; federal and state unemployment – FUTA & SUTA; workers' compensation; health insurance benefits and other applicable employer expenses and related payroll expenses).

If you are preparing a multi-year budget, subsequent years should reflect a reasonable increase of 3% to 7% per year in personnel salaries to account for anticipated annual increases for staff.

Operating Expenses include all non-personnel expenses. These items may be listed alphabetically or grouped by category with related expenses.

FTE's (Full-time equivalent)

Some grants request that the "FTE" for each staff position is stated in the application. *FTE* is used to indicate *"Full-Time Equivalent"* or *"Full-Time Employee(s)"*, an acronym used to indicate the portion of a full-time position for which a job is designed to schedule staff. The calculation is usually based on a 40 hour work week. If a reduced full-time workweek of fewer than 40 hours is used (i.e. 30 or 35 hours), this information should be clearly indicated in the budget sections of your proposal. The following chart provides examples of how FTE's are calculated.

Table 11

Sample Calculation of FTE's			
Personnel **Staff Line Item**	**Hours Planned/ Budgeted**	**Calculation**	**Total FTE's**
1 Nurse	40 per week	40/40 hrs =	1.0 FTE
1 Tutor	20 per week	20/40 hrs =	.5 FTE
1 Counselor	10 per week	10/40 hrs =	.25 FTE
2 Facilitators:	40 per week	40/40 hrs =	1.0 FTE
	10 per week	10/40 hrs =	.25 FTE
Facilitators:		**Total:**	**1.25 FTE**
3 Admin. Assts:	30 per week	30/40 hrs =	.75 FTE
	20 per week	20/40 hrs =	.5 FTE
	10 per week	10/40 hrs =	.25 FTE
Admin. Assts:		**Total:**	**1.50 FTE**
		Grand Total:	**4.50 FTE**

*If all of the positions in the chart above were for a single organization or program, the total staff FTE's for the program would equal **4.5 FTE's (1.0 + .5 + .25 + 1.25 + 1.5)**.

132

Wage and Salary Calculations Worksheet

Typically, salaries will be calculated as an annual amount. The following examples show the calculation of the hourly, weekly, monthly and annual salary for a position that pays $18.00 per hour. *You can use this the formulas on worksheet to calculate the pay for any of the time periods by using amounts specific to your program.*

1. Converting an hourly rate to a weekly rate

Weekly Salary

Hourly salary x 40 hours weekly = | $ |

Example: $18/hr x 40 hrs =$720 weekly salary

2. Converting an hourly rate to an annual salary

Annual Salary

Hourly salary x 2080 hours = | $ |

Example: $18/hr x 2080 hrs =$37,440 annual salary

3. Converting an annual salary into a monthly salary

Monthly Salary

Annual salary / 12 months = | $ |

Example: $37,440 / 12 mos. = $3,120 monthly salary

4. Converting a monthly rate into an hourly rate

Hourly Rate

Monthly salary x 12 months / 2080 hours | $ |

Example: $3,120 x 12 mos. / 2080 hrs = $18 per hour

5. Converting a monthly rate into a weekly rate

Weekly Salary

Monthly salary x 12 mos. / 52 wks = weekly salary | $ |

Example: $18/hr x 40 hrs =$720 weekly salary

6. Converting an hourly rate to a weekly rate

Weekly Salary

Weekly salary x 520 weeks = | $ |

Example: $720 x 52 wks = $37,440 annual salary

Note: Consultants and independent contractors should not be listed in the personnel section of the budget. These positions are included in the **Operating Expenses** section, usually indicated by the heading, *Consultants*.

Common Budget Considerations & Terms

The following are routinely required as a part of the grant application:

Total organizational budget – also referred to as the "annual agency budget," most funders require this budget to be included with the proposal. This also applies when the proposal is for a specific program. This allows the funder to assess how the proposed project fits into the overall budget and programming for the organization

List of past and/or current funding sources – some funders request a roster of other funding sources that have provided support for your organization. The request is typically for a list that includes funding support for the current year and may require this information for one or more prior years. Some funders also request a list of "pending" funding requests. Funders don't use this information to penalize applicants. In contrast, they may use the information to determine if you are among "pending" applicants their colleagues may be giving serious consideration for a grant. Funders sometimes engage in discussions about the amount they may consider awarding to the same applicant. This sometimes results in the coordination of their mutual support to provide some level of grant award from their respective funds for agencies and programs they have deemed effective.

Other common requests related to your organization's funding history include:

- A list of sources that have provided the largest amounts of funding. This type of request usually requires the name of the funder, amount given, purpose, and the grant period (i.e. "10 largest funders for the past two years").

- All grants in excess of a certain amount during a specific time period (i.e. "all grants in excess of $20,000")

Sustainability – What are the plans to secure future funding? Many funders want to know your plans for maintaining the program in the future without relying on repeat funding from them.

Inkind

Donations of time, services and other resources are referred to as *inkind*. The dollar value applied to donated services should reflect a reasonable market value for the specific inkind donation. Two examples are provided below:

Example A: If an accountant agrees to donate services for 10 hours a week on a monthly basis, the amount they would normally charge for the service should be included in the budget and identified as *inkind*.

Example B: If a local restaurant donates food for a client awards ceremony, the amount they would have normally charged for the food should be included in the budget and identified as *inkind*.

Program Expenses (sometimes referred to as "Operating Expenses")

This category includes all resources needed to support programs and/or services that provide a direct benefit to clients. These are routinely referred to as expenses for "direct services." Two examples are provided below:

Example: (staff/personnel expenses): a recreation leader who supervises children during activities; a counselor who meets with clients; an intake worker who assists clients with completing paperwork to enroll in the agency's programs.

Example: (program expenses): notebooks for tutoring program; video screen used for program arts presentations; printed brochures used for outreach to inform the community of services.

Some government and foundation funders forbid the purchase of equipment with grant funds, but sometimes allow these items to be leased. The application instructions will always stipulate the restrictions regarding the purchase of equipment or other items. Restrictions will always be stipulated in the written grant agreement that must be signed as a condition of receiving funds. Your program is likely to have some line items that are unique to your program. For example, a summer oceanography program may include a *Boat Rental* line item for field trip activities. A program for teenage mothers may include a *Child Care/Babysitting* line item. Refer to page139 for a list of line items commonly found in many program budgets.

Administrative Expenses is a category of expenses used for staff and all other resources that are not used in the direct service of clients. Although the program would not be able to operate without these resources, they are not considered "program expenses" and are usually limited to a maximum of 5% to 15% of the total project budget. Administrative expenses are also referred to as "Administrative Overhead" or "Overhead." As of the publication of this workbook, the federal government allows applicants and grantees to apply a rate up to 12%* to calculate Administrative Expenses. Many funders use the federal rate as a frame of reference to inform their respective rates. See examples below:

Example A: The monthly bill for a telephone used by the bookkeeper is classified as an administrative expense, but a telephone placed in a job search library to be used by clients is considered a direct service expense.

Example B: Office supplies used by the executive director and office staff are classified as administrative expenses, but office supplies used by the clients during the program activities are considered direct service expenses.

---

*The rate is sometimes applied to the Personnel Subtotal before the addition of employer taxes or benefits, however it is sometimes applied to the total of all expenses.

Indirect Expenses is a term sometimes used interchangeably in the nonprofit sector to refer to Administrative Expenses. However, there is a technical and practical distinction when the term applies to government grants. For federal grants, the applicant agency must obtain an approved rate for Indirect Expenses. The rate is obtained through a standard application and negotiation process. Once approved, the agency can apply this rate to budgets submitted for all federal grants.

Nonprofits with annual budgets of less than $2 million rarely pursue this option unless they have a heavy reliance on federal grants to cover a significant portion of their annual budget.

Organizations may develop their own formulas to calculate a rate for Administrative Overhead. The rate may be based on the percent of total square footage used by each program, an allocation of expenses based on the number of staff, a percent of total facility expenses or other measurements.

Developing The Annual Budget

Once you have finished recording staff and operational expenses on the worksheets (for your overall agency, or a specific program), you will have all the information needed to prepare the annual budget. You will need to estimate and calculate each line item expense for a twelve-month period. The only exception is for projects with time frames of less than 12 months (i.e. summer program or one-time project that will be completed in less than twelve months, or a specific time period stipulated by the funder).

Be mindful of upfront expenses for certain line items (i.e. cost of telephone or other equipment and initial installation; annual amount needed to cover monthly service contract for a copy machine or other equipment). This will ensure the budget includes amounts sufficient to cover all expenses required for the proposed program.

————

Some applications require a budget <u>and</u> a line item justification (or budget narrative). The term "budget justification" most commonly refers to a "line item justification," however, it is sometimes used to refer to a "budget narrative." Pay attention to the funders' instructions so that you will make the appropriate decision regarding which format to prepare.

A line item justification provides a brief description of the specific purpose for each *line item** included in the budget. Instructions, a sample and a worksheet are on pages 144-146. A budget narrative describes the purpose of the expenses and is usually written in a paragraph format. See pages 147-149 for a sample and worksheet.

Worksheets on the following pages will make it easy to document all of the costs associated with your program. After you complete the set of budget sheets, the information can be consolidated into a one or two page budget document using spreadsheet software. Later you will be able to "cut & paste" line items onto any application form as needed.

Exercise 13 – Developing The Budget

Using the summary budget information from your completed **Program Design Worksheet** from Exercise 7 (page 94), add details to develop the line items on the following **Budget Worksheet** for the personnel and operating expenses needed to operate the program.

Information and the *worksheet* for preparing the **Personnel** section of the budget can be found on pages 131–133 and *138*; for **Operating Expenses**, see pages 131, 135-136 and *140-144*.

---

line item is the term used to refer to each budget item that has been assigned a dollar amount.

Budget Worksheet
(Page 1 of 4)

I. Personnel - Wages & Salaries

List each part-time and full-time paid position that will be needed to operate the program. Refer to page 132 for an explanation and overview of FTE's.)

	FTE	12-Month Budget
1.		$
2.		$
3.		$
4.		$
5.		$
6.		$
7.		$
8.		$
9.		$
10.		$
11.		$
12.		$
13.		$
14.		$
15.		$
16.		
17.		
18.		
19.		
20.		
Total Wages & Salaries/FTE's:		$
Employer Payroll Taxes & Benefits (25%):		$
Total Personnel:		$
TOTAL STAFF WAGES:		$
BENEFITS @ 25%*:		$
TOTAL PROGRAM STAFF BUDGET:		$

*At the time of publication, this rate reflects an estimated, average for mandatory employer payroll taxes, health insurance premiums and other expenses related to employee compensation.

Common Budget Line Items

Worksheets on the following pages can be used to record operating expenses for your program. Your budget information can be transferred to standard forms that a funder may provide as part of the application. If no forms are provided, it is appropriate to list expenses either by category or alphabetically.

The budget worksheet on page 142 is designed with sections to create additional budget categories as needed. An extra blank worksheet on page 143 can be used to list the budget line items in the order most appropriate for your organization. The following list contains expenses common to many programs. This list is intended to serve as prompt to help you get started. You will likely need to add additional items specific to your program.

Accounting/Bookkeeping	Office Supplies
Administrative*	Outreach Activities
Advertising	Payroll Service
Audit Expenses	Payroll Taxes
Bank Fees	Personnel (staff salaries/wages)
Computer Maintenance	Postage/Overnight Delivery/Courier
Computer System	Printing
Computer Software	Program Supplies
Consultants/Professional Services	Rent/Lease
Conference Fees	Security
Dues & Subscriptions	Social Media Services
Equipment	Staff Training
Facility Cleaning/Maintenance	Subscriptions
Furniture & Fixtures	Telecommunications (phone, WiFi)
Insurance	Telephone Equipment
I.T. Services & Support	Transportation
Leasehold Improvements	Travel
Legal Fees	Utilities
Licenses/Permits	Vendor Credit Card Fees
Mileage	Website Maintenance

---

*Unless you have already determined a rate to calculate this line item, 10% of the total program budget is recommended for the *Administrative Expenses* line item This will be used for overhead expenses that are impractical to calculate, as they may apply to numerous line items. Although some funders don't fund administrative or "general operating" expenses, it is important to calculate and include this line item in your budget to ensure that your budget reflects the full cost of operating your agency and programs.

Budget Worksheet
(Page 2 of 4)

II. Operating Expenses	12 Month Budget
Facility:	
	$
Total Facility Expenses:	$
Computers & I.T. Services:	
	$
Total Computers & I.T.:	$
Furniture & Equipment:	
	$
Total Furniture & Equipment:	$
Marketing & Communications:	
Total Marketing & Communications:	$
CONTINUED ON NEXT PAGE	

Budget Worksheet
(Page 3 of 4)

II. Operating Expenses	12 Month Budget
Materials & Supplies:	
	$
Total Materials & Supplies:	$
Travel, Transportation & Mileage:	
Total Travel, Transportation & Mileage:	
Professional Services & Consultants:	
	$
Total Professional Services & Consultants	$
Legal Fees, Permits & Licenses:	
	$
Total Legal Fees, Permits & Licenses:	$

CONTINUED ON NEXT PAGE

Budget Worksheet
(Page 4 of 4)

12 Month Budget

III. Other:

Use this page to record all other expenses. You may wish to make extra copies to create a separate page for categories to group similar items or expenses (i.e. Outreach Activities, Job Fair). It may also be used to prepare a line item specific to a particular program, special project or location where services will be provided.

Other A:	
	$
Total Other - A:	$
Other B:	
	$
Total Other - B:	$
Other C:	
	$
Total Other - C:	
	$
TOTAL BUDGET*:	$

FINAL PAGE(S) OF BUDGET WORKSHEET

*Combined totals from all pages of the budget worksheets: (Page 1) Personnel + Computers & I.T., Furniture & Equipment + Marketing & Communications + (Page 3) Materials & Supplies + Travel, Tourism & Mileage + Professional Services & Consulting + Legal Fees, Permits & Licenses + (Page 4) Other

If applicable, add totals from any additional Budget Worksheets completed using the form on page 143.

Budget Worksheet

Page _____ of _____

Title/Category: _____

12 Month Budget

Use this page to record all other expenses in the order and/or categories most suited to the needs of your organization. Make blank copies as needed.

	$
TOTAL BUDGET*:	$

*Add this amount to the totals on pages 1 thru 4 to calculate the total budget.

FINAL PAGE(S) OF BUDGET WORKSHEET

The Budget Justification

Some applications require a budget justification, which may be referred to as a "line item justification." It provides a brief description of the purpose for each line item, and should include:

1) The name or description of the line item,

2) The budgeted amount,

3) A brief description of the purpose for the item in the program, and

4) A summary calculation for the line item

It is important to prepare this document for your program even if it is not required by the funding source. In addition to providing details about how the cost for each item is calculated, it will also serve as a convenient frame of reference for further program development and other management uses.

The *justification* may be included on the same page as the budget if space permits. The sample on the following page is for the Community Resource Center, with an annual budget of $142,626. A worksheet is provided on page 146. Unless the funder provides a standard form, the justification may be prepared on a sheet separate from the budget (refer to the sample budget justifications on pages 108-109 and 145.

A brief overview of the *budget narrative* and a sample are provided on page 147-148.

Exercise 14 – Preparing the Budget Justification

Instructions: After reviewing the following sample justification, complete the **Budget Justification Worksheet** on page 146 for your program.

Budget Justification
Community Resource Center

1 Program Director (.5 FTE*) $36,000 yr x 50% of full-time	$ 18,000	Responsible for coordinating all facets of the program, including administration, training and supervision of program
3 Group Coordinators (1.5 FTE*) $12K each per yr)	$ 36,000	Conduct community outreach, facilitate group counseling sessions and assist participants in obtaining complementary services from other local organizations
1 Administrative Asst. (1 FTE*) $2,000 mo. X 12 mos.	$ 24,000	Answer phones, provide information, prepare correspondence and maintain filing system for administrative and client activitie.
Payroll Taxes/Benefits ($78K total salaries x 22%)	$ 17,160	Payroll taxes and health insurance premiums for full-time Administrative Assistant
Rent (**2,400** x $1.20 sq. ft.)	$ 28,800	Annual expense for **2,400** sq. ft. facility office and program
Utilities ($300/mo. X 12 mos.)	$ 3,600	Electricity, gas and water
Computer Equipment (3 x $700 each)	$ 2,100	3 computers & 3 color inkjet printers: One for Administrative Assistant, two in learning center

TOTAL:	$129,660
ADMINISTRATIVE OVERHEAD (10%):	$ 12,966
TOTAL PROGRAM **BUDGET:**	**$ 142,626**

---

*A description of FTE's is included on page 132.

Budget Justification Worksheet

Budgeted Line Item	Amount*	Justification How does this item support the program? Why is this item important or needed? Also, record the calculation for each line item.

*Prepare a separate worksheet that includes details and any notes used to calculate each budget item. File it for future reference. Prepare a succinct, summary of the calculation to place immediately following the brief justification for each item.

The Budget Narrative

As the name implies, the *budget narrative* is written in narrative form and describes the overall budget and how it relates to the program described in the proposal. Both the *budget narrative* and the *line item justification* are prepared to accompany grant budgets, but funders usually request only one format. It is important to prepare the more detailed *line item justification* for your own reference, even if the funder does not request it. There are similarities and differences between the two, as reflected in the following highlights that pertain to the b*udget narrative*, which:

- Unlike the *budget justification*, this document does not include a list of individual line items nor their respective calculations. It may include some references to amounts and percentages (see sample on the following page),

- Serves the purpose of providing a general overview of how funds will be used to support the program described in the proposal, and

- Should be limited to a maximum of 1-2 pages unless other details are requested by the funder's application instructions.

A budget narrative should emphasize how the grant would be put to good use. It should convey the soundness and appropriateness of the overall budget to support the success of the program.

Some funders require applicants to indicate the exact line item(s) for which the grant is requested. In this instance, focus on and highlight how and why the specific item(s) are important to the success of the program.

Begin by crafting an introduction to the specific program proposed for funding. If your budget includes personnel, provide an overview of the staff positions or categories and a brief description of their roles within the proposed program.

Next, prepare an overview of operational expenses to highlight strengths and unique aspects of the program as much as possible. Finally, include an explanation of how the amount for administrative overhead was calculated.

The budget narrative for the "Community Resource Center" is on the next page. It was prepared to provide an example of the narrative format of the earlier sample budget justification presented on page 145.

(SAMPLE)
Community Resource Center
Budget Narrative

A grant from Mucho Dinero Foundation will be used to support staffing and program activities at the Community Resource Center operated by (Name of Organization) in downtown Sweezena, Maryland. These funds will be used to expand services by providing funds to increase the current part-time director to full-time. It will also allow us to staff the program with two, full-time group coordinators by increasing hours for our current staff of one part-time coordinator to full-time. One additional, full-time group coordinator with a certificate in counseling will be hired to oversee the scheduling of one-on-one counseling sessions and referrals for mental health services. The additional staff will accommodate the anticipated increase in the number of seniors who will enroll for services over the next twelve months.

The facility space supported by this grant includes office space for the three staff described in the proposal. It includes two small offices, one for the director and one shared by the coordinators. The space includes one small meeting room to provide privacy for individual counseling session. It also includes two large community rooms that can be used for group activities. Space allocated for these program activities accounts for only 20% of the total square footage of the Center.

Three new computers and printers will be purchased for the program. One of the systems will replace an outdated computer used by the administrative assistant. This individual is responsible for completing all enrollment and registration forms for seniors who utilize the Center. Funded by other sources, this individual also maintains the database of client information. The other computer equipment will be set-up in the computer lab/learning center. The lab will have a total of 18 computer stations with the addition of the new systems. Our computers are heavily used throughout the week, including weekly group trainings for seniors and after-school tutoring and activities for children and families. During the evening we offer for-fee workshops, which generated $7,000 last year.

Our agency applies a flat 10% rate of the program budget for administrative overhead.

Exercise 15 – Preparing the Budget Narrative

Instructions: Use the completed **Budget Justification Worksheet** from Exercise 14 (page 144) to prepare a budget narrative using the worksheet on the following page.

Budget Narrative Worksheet

Name of program (if applicable): _____

Name of organization: _____

Introduction:

Summary description and highlights related to Personnel:

Summary description and highlights related to Operational and Program:

Succinct description, rationale or reference for your calculation of Administrative Overhead and/or Indirect expenses:

Part VII: Workplan
aka "Scope of Work" (SOW) or "Timeline"

This section provides an overview of formats most commonly used for timelines prepared to accompany grant applications. It also covers the process, provides examples and includes instructions on how this document is prepared.

After completion of this section, you should be able to prepare a workplan that will:

- Be the most appropriate for the proposal(s) to be prepared and submitted

- Indicate how your program will be implemented

- Identify, develop and describe quantitative outcomes and deliverables for your programs to include in your grant proposals

- Serve as a useful guide for the implementation of key components of the proposed program, within specific time periods

- Clearly align with the proposal narrative and budget

As you proceed with the completion of exercises in this workbook, concurrently it is important to begin the process of collecting and recording information onto the **Master Grant Data Worksheet** (Pages 180-231). If you will follow this recommendation, you will have all of the information needed to prepare any type of grant application by the time you complete this workbook.

Workplan Overview

A workplan provides a snapshot of the entire schedule for the implementation (or ongoing operation) of the program. This document is also routinely referred to as a *Timeline* or *Scope of Work (SOW)*, with the latter more commonly required for government grants. Preparing this document will help you think through the sequential steps needed to implement and operate your program. It should include key tasks that indicate an appropriate level of movement or progress needed to plan, implement, expand or maintain the agency (or program).

Some applications require the preparation of a **Scope of Work (SOW),** which is commonly included as an Attachment. It typically stipulates **what** is going to be done, **when**, by **whom** and the **evaluation** method that will be used to determine program progress or success. This is the type of timeline/workplan most often required by government funders. Most funders will provide specific instructions regarding the content and format should an SOW be required.

A workplan always includes a list of key *deliverables* or *outcomes*, which are the milestones or measurable goals expected to be achieved as a result of the program.

Each *deliverable* placed on the workplan should be:

- Clearly identified and should be a component, process or activity that is key to the program's success,

- An item to which some type of quantitative measure can be applied (which may relate to being completed within a certain timeframe, or may be a measurement that shows sequential progress towards specific objectives or milestones), and

- Assigned a date for completion, or measurable progression within a specific timeframe.

This document is used to show how the program described in the proposal would be implemented if funded. It should be prepared with a focus on the main components and key activities needed to ensure the progress and success of the program. It is imperative to establish a projected deadline date for the completion of each of these elements.

> Once a grant is awarded, the workplan becomes part of the grant agreement

Finally, every item noted on the workplan must be aligned with details included in all other sections of the proposal. When the workplan is completed, the connection to the program description, goals and objectives, and budget should be clear. It would be futile to include items on a workplan that have not been addressed elsewhere in the proposal. A well-developed workplan can be used as part of the tracking and assessment process after the proposal is funded. When a grant is funded for an amount lower than what was requested, the workplan usually has to be modified, as it becomes part of the formal grant agreement.

A Variety of Workplan Formats

With the exception of e-apps that require the entry of workplan information into data fields, this document can be created in a variety of formats. For some proposals, the format of the workplan will be dictated by the funder. In these instances, their grant guidelines will include an actual form, a template or a sample to use as a guide to prepare the workplan. The most important thing to get started is to know which categories of information need to be included on the workplan. Four commonly used formats for workplans are described below, with a sample of each on subsequent pages in the remainder of this section.

Narrative (basic paragraph format)
Presented in a basic paragraph format, this style is appropriate for e-apps that provide a single data field with limited space to enter the entire workplan. See page 154 for Sample A and additional information.

Basic List or **Bulletpoints**
This format presents the same information in a more user-friendly layout and is appropriate for hard copy applications or for e-apps that request the workplan as an attachment. See page 155 for Sample B and additional information.

Gantt Chart
This format is designed with all of the main components in a layout that makes it easy to review them alongside their respective timelines. An electronic spreadsheet can be used to prepare this format if you do not have access to project management software. Key components are listed along the left margin. A series of checkmarks or shaded cells can be used to indicate the projected progress for each component. This style is appropriate for a hard copy application or for e-apps that request the workplan as an attachment. See page 156 for Sample C and additional information.

Scope of Work (SOW)
This format is most commonly requested by government funding sources and includes more detail than the other formats. This style usually requires the preparation of multiple pages to record details for each key deliverable or outcome. *Some funders may provide a sample SOW to use as a guide, or a blank template or form.* This style is appropriate for a hard copy application or for e-apps that request the workplan as an attachment. See pages 158-159 for additional information and Sample D.

The following samples have been prepared for a counseling program for delinquent youth. In order to present one sample per page, each one includes major tasks for a period of at least four months. The remaining months and major tasks would be added to complete the timeline for the standard funding cycle of at least 12 months.

When there are no instructions, it is acceptable to limit the workplan to 1-2 pages, keeping it as simple and as concise as possible. You may structure the timeline in increments of months, days, quarters, seasons, etc. This will make it easy to reference the time increments and overall time line to be applied to the implementation and completion of tasks and activities for your program.

SAMPLE A – **Narrative (Basic Paragraph) Format**

This format is appropriate for e-apps that provide a single data field with limited space to enter the entire workplan. It can be prepared for e-apps that do <u>not</u> allow the *Workplan* to be uploaded as a separate attachment.

As of the publication of this workbook, existing e-app systems do <u>not</u> allow basic text formatting features like using **bold**, <u>underline</u>, *italic* or the use of bullet points. You can use all capital letters to make the visual distinction when introducing a new section (see how each month is introduced in the sample below).

If there is enough room in the data field, you can begin each new month on a separate line and use all capital letters or substitute the use of hyphens for bullet points.

SAMPLE A
Counseling Program for Delinquent Youth: Year 1 Timeline/Workplan

MONTH 1 - Sign facility lease & purchase furnishings, obtain required licenses and permits, develop and distribute outreach materials to collaborators and hire program coordinator. MONTH 2 - Schedule meeting with local law enforcement & mayor, begin registration for participants, order program materials, hire program counselors and conduct staff training. MONTH 3 - Conduct orientation for participants, begin program activities and make arrangements for participants to attend state conference. MONTH 4 - Recruit volunteer peer-counselors, host luncheon for mayor to speak to participants and assign participants to community service locations. MONTH 5 .... *(continue recording the activities through MONTH 12 in the same manner).*

Note: Some e-app systems will automatically delete blank spaces between lines when an application is saved in the final format for online submission, so it is important to make the beginning of different sections clear. See a modification of Sample A below:

- Month 1: Sign facility lease & purchase furnishings, obtain required licenses and permits, develop and distribute outreach materials to collaborators and hire program coordinator
- Month 2: Schedule meeting with local law enforcement & mayor, begin registration for participants, order program materials, hire program counselors and conduct staff training
- Month 3: Conduct orientation for participants, begin program activities and make arrangements for participants to attend state conference
- Month 4: Recruit volunteer peer-counselors, host luncheon for mayor to speak to participants and assign participants to community service locations
- Month 5: .... *(continue with recording of activities through Month 12)*

SAMPLE B – **Basic List or Bullet Point Format**

This layout makes it easier to read and locate the individual items on the workplan. This is an appropriate format to include with a hard copy application or for any online application that allows the workplan to be uploaded as an attachment.

(SAMPLE B)
Counseling Program for Delinquent Youth
Timeline/Workplan
Year 1

Month 1
- Sign facility lease & purchase furnishings
- Obtain required licenses and permits
- Develop and distribute outreach materials to collaborators
- Hire program coordinator

Month 2
- Schedule meeting with local law enforcement & mayor
- Registration for participants
- Order program materials
- Hire program counselors
- Conduct staff training

Month 3
- Conduct orientation for participants
- Begin program activities
- Make arrangements for participants to attend state conference

Month 4
- Recruit volunteer peer-counselors
- Host luncheon for mayor to speak to participants
- Assign participants to community service locations

Month 5 ..... *Continue recording activities for months 6-12. Use extra pages as needed*

SAMPLE C – **Gantt Chart**

Historically associated with the fields of engineering and business, variations of this format are commonly known as Gantt Charts. It is named after Henry Laurence Gantt, an American mechanical engineer and management consultant credited with creating this style of chart in the early 1900's.

Year 1 Workplan: Counseling Program for Delinquent Youth

Month -->	1	2	3	4	5	6...	...12
Administrative							
Sign facility lease	X						
Purchase facility furnishings	X						
Obtain licenses & permits	X						
Staffing & Personnel							
Hire program counselors		XXX		X			
Recruit peer-counselors			X				
Conduct staff training		X					
Begin participant registration			X				
Participant orientation (monthly thru Month 8)			X	X	X	X	
Marketing/Outreach							
Design and order program materials	X						
Distribute outreach materials to collaborators			XXXX				
Program Activities							
Meeting w/local law enforcement and mayor				X			
Commence program activities			X	XXXX	XXXX	XXXX	
Assign participants to locations (Months 5-8)					X	X	
Host luncheon (w/mayor as guest speaker)						X	
Finalize travel & registration for state conference						X	

Notes:

1. Items in the list have been grouped into categories based on the type of activity
  (i.e. Administrative, Staffing & Personnel, Marketing/Outreach and Program Activities)

2. Columns for Months 5 & 6 have been added to demonstrate how some activities are ongoing.

3. Each monthly column for this sample has four (4) spaces. This allows the placement of the "X's" to coincide with the beginning, middle or end of each month, which provides a convenient visual reference for when items are expected to be completed.

Exercise 16 – Preparing the Workplan

Instructions: Using information from Exercise 10 (page 121), complete the Timeline/Workplan Worksheet on the following page by listing the major tasks required to establish and implement the program within a reasonable sequence and time frame.

Timeline/Workplan Worksheet	
Timeframe for Action*	Prepare a List or Brief Description of Key Program Components *(may include measurable outcomes, objectives or tangible deliverables)*

*This worksheet is designed with four rows to make it easy to develop an annual timeline in quarterly increments. However, you can prepare the timeline using any increments you determine appropriate for your program.

Scope of Work (aka "Scope" or "SOW")

A Scope of Work (SOW) is prepared for work to be performed on projects funded by grants, contracts or subcontracts. Due to the range of applications, there is no standard format for a Scope. Some are prepared in an outline, narrative form with a heading to introduce each section. Some are prepared in a tabular format, similar to Sample B on page 155; however a Scope will include additional details as referenced by the list of bullet points on this page.

A Scope document is usually required for RFP's issued by government entities. It should include every key component or activity needed to implement and complete the project described in the proposal. This includes a list of specific tasks and deadlines for their completion.

The total pages are contingent upon the number of key components and related details that need to be included. If the funder's application does not provide guidelines, answer the following set of questions to ensure the development of a good Scope:

- What are the major components that need to be put in place or completed for he successful implementation of the program? *This will include goals, measurable objectives and any deliverables that will be produced as a result of the funding.*

- Who is responsible for each component? *Different individuals may be responsible for different components.*

- When is the deadline for completing each component? *Determine specific dates for each component. Some are ongoing.*

- What is the process for implementing the program? *Information specific to each component should be listed.*

- How will you determine when the program is completed? *This should specify what will determine the completion of each major component.*

- What is the cost? *For components that have a related budget line item, identify the amount.*

For proposals selected for funding, the grantee may be required to modify the workplan to include information regarding due dates for reports, invoices and other deliverables. A sample of a partial Scope of Work is included on the following page.

		(SAMPLE D)	
Scope of Work: Counseling Program for Delinquent Youth (Year 1)			
Area of Focus	**Milestone(s) or Deliverable(s)**	**Estimated Completion Date or Deadline**	**Indicate Department/ and Individual Responsible**
Outreach Materials	Design and order outreach materials	Month 1: 3/15	Development Department/Outreach Coordinator
	Distribute materials to collaborators	Month 1: 3/31	Client Services/Outreach Supervisor
Staffing	Hire program coordinator	Month 2: 4/15	Executive Director
	Conduct staff training	Month 2: 4/30	Human Resources Consultant
	Recruit volunteer peer counselors	Month 4: 6/15	Client Services Director
Program Implementation	Sign lease and furnish facility	Month 1: 3/31	Executive Director
	Register participants	Month 2: 4/30	Client Services Department/Case Manager Supervisor
	Participant luncheon	Month 4: 6/30	Executive Director
Invoices and Reports	Prepare/Submit invoice and narrative program report	Monthly (due by 10th of month following activity)	Executive Director

There is no standard format for a Scope of Work. Some are prepared in an outline format with headings to introduce each major section. Sample D is one example of a style prepared in a table format, with a portrait orientation. Some SOW's are prepared in landscape format and may require multiple pages to accommodate all of the detail needed. This type of layout can be prepared with a spreadsheet like MS Excel® or the table feature in a program like MS Word®.

A brief description of each of the four column headings used to prepare this sample is provided: **Area of Focus** - List additional areas of focus as appropriate; **Milestone(s) or Deliverable(s)** - Select and record major goals and/or measurable objectives; **Estimated Completion Date or Deadline** - Indicate date the task will be completed; **Indicate Department and Individual Responsible** - List department names and the job titles (and/or names) of the individuals responsible for the completion of tasks needed to achieve the milestone or deliverable.

E-MAIL

VIII: Packaging and Submitting the Grant Application

This section provides an overview of the most commonly used methods to package and submit grant applications, both hard copy and online.

After completion of this section, you should be able to:

- Use a checklist to confirm that your proposal includes everything required by a funder

- Organize all of the required documents to submit according to a funder's instructions

- Submit a professionally-prepared proposal

VIII: Packaging and Submitting the Grant Application

You've finished the grant, now what? Congratulations for your persistence and hard work. Finally it's time to compile all of the required documents into a completed application packet, hardcopy or digital. Follow the seven-steps below to complete the process appropriate for your specific application.

Step 1:   Submit your grant proposal on time!

Online Submissions: Be aware of different time zones. Deadlines stated in funders' guidelines refer to their respective time zones. A New York based funder may or may not indicate its deadline as Eastern Standard Time (EST), which could make a difference if you are located in Texas and need to work on your application until the last possible minute. In this instance, you would need to factor in the time difference to meet the deadline. Due to the time difference, an 11:00pm online submission from an agency in California for an April 30th deadline would be two hours too late to meet the April 30th deadline for a funder located in Washington, D.C.

Hard copy applications: Confirm the funder's deadline. Is it the postmark date or a "must arrive in the funder's office by a specific date and time"? Determine the actual deadline and plan your mailing or other delivery method accordingly.

Step 2:   Verify your proposal is complete

Print a copy of the **Grant Proposal Development Outline** (page 83) that you prepared for the specific funding request. Use the outline as a checklist to determine if your application is complete.

Step 3:   Prepare attachments

Pay close attention to the list of attachments required. Confirm that all of the attachments are completed and readily accessible,

Note: Assign a file name to the proposal and all related documents that will make identification easy for future reference. This also includes worksheets and other files used to develop the proposal. Some funders will provide instructions for file names.

Online applications: Use the **Roster of Commonly Requested Attachments Worksheet** (pages 229-230) to record the file name(s) and location(s) of your digital files that contain attachments. These files need to be readily accessible for you to upload to online systems as attachments.

Hardcopy applications: Print a hard copy of all attachments required. You need to have these documents readily available to prepare your packet for mailing.

If applicable, make the correct number of copies required by the funder. Remember to make at least one extra copy of the proposal narrative for your files. However, it is not necessary to make copies of any attachments that you already maintain in files to use on a regular basis (i.e. IRS Letter, 990 Tax Form).

Step 4: Package the application

Online applications:

The funder's **E-app** system will guide you through each step needed to attach files including any special instructions regarding file names to use for attachments, etc.

For **online apps** that require all files as attachments, follow guidelines for formatting. Do they request individual text documents for narrative info, spreadsheet files for financial information? Or have they requested a single file that contains the entire proposal in .pdf format?

Note: If a .pdf format is required, you will need to save or scan your documents as a .pdf file.

Hardcopy applications:

Package the grant application according to the funder's instructions. Follow guidelines for the number of copies, original signatures on standard forms, etc. Pay attention to their "Do not" lists (i.e. "no staples," no binding" or "no extra documents" other than what is indicated as their instructions).

Unless the funder expressly states that no other documents are to be included with the proposal, it is appropriate to prepare a brief, one-page maximum, **cover letter** on the applicant agency's letterhead. It is also appropriate to include a program brochure or newsletter. Instructions, a sample cover letter and worksheet are provided on pages 166-168.

Step 5: Submit the application

Online applications: Follow all instructions, which will entail uploading the required attachments, then follow the system's instructions to submit the application. You will receive an auto-reply message indicating that your application has been received. It will include instructions for any other follow-up required. Some systems will also send a confirmation of receipt to the e-mail initially registered for access to the online system.

Hardcopy applications: At this point you should be ready to mail your completed proposal or have it delivered by other appropriate means (courier, overnight or in-person delivery). It is a good practice to use Certified Mail or some other method that will provide proof of delivery and/or receipt (i.e. overnight courier, return receipt). This is especially important if you are mailing it close to the deadline. You always want to ensure that you will have time to confirm that your proposal has been received in time to meet the deadline.

Step 6: After submitting the application

The instructions for this step apply to all applications.

Use the **Grant Application Tracking & Status Form** to record the submission of the proposal. You can use this form as part of a system to schedule follow-up as needed (see page 171).

File each completed proposal along with the application instructions and all worksheets, including the budget calculations. Most nonprofits maintain both the hard copy and digital file of each application in some type of filing system for easy retrieval.

The recommended order for filing the proposal documents is noted below. Items 1–5 comprise a copy of the full application packet for your convenient reference

1. Copy of full proposal (with the cover letter on top, if applicable)

2. Application guidelines/instructions

3. Budget(s)

    a. Agency budget – you may include a copy of the agency budget <u>or</u> notes indicating the file name (and location for convenient reference or retrieval) of the specific budget that was submitted

    b. Program budget, if applicable

4. Attachments – Prepare a list with file names and locations of the attachments that you maintain and use on a routine basis. It is not necessary to include copies of documents that you keep on file.   Make a hard copy of the attachments that are specific to the grant request and place them in the file with the grant proposal (i.e. program budget, MOU or agreement letter from a collaborating agency included with the proposal). This will make it convenient to retrieve and respond to any requests for additional information from the funder in a timely manner.

5. Budget worksheets and notes – the worksheets and related notes that you used to develop and calculate the budget and other important details should be compiled and filed at the back of the proposal packet.

6. Communications Log - to document and track all categories of communication between you and the funder (including the date along with any notes regarding the content of phone calls and meetings). Emails, letters and other written communication can be recorded with a reference to the date, subject and any pertinent details to highlight the purpose or significance of the correspondence.

Step 7: Proceed with the preparation of your next grant proposal

Congratulations! If you have followed the steps to submit a grant application, you are obviously willing to invest the time and effort to secure grant awards. Next steps?

First, select two additional funding sources appropriate to prepare applications for the grant request you just completed.

Second, follow the step-by-step process to develop two more proposal(s). Save time by using your completed proposal as a template; you can edit it as needed to adhere to the guidelines for the new funding sources.

Third, submit and file the proposals.

This strategy is recommended to jump start your efforts. It is important to keep grant applications in the pipeline. You will greatly increase the probability and frequency of securing grant awards by adopting this strategy.

Grant Proposal Cover Letter

Typically applicable to hard copy applications, the cover letter is usually the last document prepared after the proposal has been completed. It should be concise, yet contains other important details or highlights that may tout the strength or uniqueness of your agency or program. You want to emphasize the most impressive aspects of what is included in your proposal, not waste time or space unnecessarily repeating anything that is already stated in the proposal.

This document should be kept to a maximum of one page. It should be prepared on the organization's letterhead and signed by the executive director. Some funders may require the signature of the board chair or another authorized agent of the agency.

A cover letter should include the following information:

• An introduction to your organization,

• A brief description of the program that you are proposing; in other words, for what will the funding be used?

• The total amount of funding that you are requesting in your proposal,

• Additional highlights about your agency or program that are not noted in the proposal, and

• Signature - although the letter may be signed by the board president or executive director, be sure to reference and include the name, job title and contact information for the person who will be able to answer any questions that the funder may have about the proposal or proposed program.

A sample letter is provided on the following page. A worksheet for you to prepare a cover letter is provided on page 168.

An "Executive Summary" may be required by some funders. It should provide an overview of the entire proposal and be limited to one page unless other instructions are provided.

(SAMPLE COVER LETTER)

Neighborhood Economic Development Network
2928 Main Street
Anywhere, USA 03839

President
Funders Unlimited
48380 Cashaway Lane
Prosperity, MN 88333

Dear President:

We are seeking funding support in the amount of $120,000 to establish a computer lab at the Mildway Housing Project located near downtown Anywhere. This computer lab will be a valuable resource for persons who wish to learn basic computer skills for entry-level employment positions.

Our agency has been serving homeless and low-income residents in this area for the past seven years. Our soup kitchen serves more than 300 persons each day. Our holiday events have provided hearty meals, toys for childran and gifts to more than 2,000 families during the past five seasons. The proposed program will enhance our ability to assist clients with developing basic job skills. The ultimate goal is to help them find employment and support their success in becoming self-sufficient.

We appreciate the opportunity to submit this proposal and encourage you to visit our website at www.NEDN.net to learn more about our programs. Please contact me, if you have any additional questions, at (732) 853-1212 or eieio@nedn.net.

Sincerely,

Travis Trailer
Executive Director

cc: Proposal
        Board list
        IRS letter
        Agency brochure

Grant Proposal Cover Letter Worksheet

Instructions: First, use the space in the right column to record a brief response/answer to each item in the left column. After you complete this step, "cut & paste" your responses onto your agency's letterhead to prepare a draft of your cover letter. Proofread and finalize for signature. If you prefer, you may record your responses to each item directly onto letterhead to prepare the initial draft.

1. Date:	
2. Name of funder's contact person: 3. Official title of contact person: 4. Name of funder: 5. Funder's mailing address: 6. City, State and Zip Code:	
Dear **(Contact)**:	
7. How much are you requesting?:	
8. What programs or activities will this grant support?:	
9. Provide a very brief description of your organization. In some instances, the mission statement may be sufficient:	
10. If this request is for a specific program, provide a brief description of the program:	
11. Prepare a closing paragraph that includes the contact information for the person at your organization who will be responsible for communicating with the funder:	
Sincerely,	
Name of signatory: **Title of signatory**:	
Enclosures: **List each document included with the proposal**	

Grant Submission Checklist

If the funder provides a checklist, be sure to incorporate their items into your **Grant Proposal Development Worksheet** (page 83). Checklists provided by funders are typically useful to verify that certain documents are included. However, their checklists are not intended to address the level of detail needed for the actual grant writing process.

If you have followed the step-by-step process presented in this workbook, you have already recorded all of the information needed on the *Master Grant Template Worksheets* (pages 184-231).

It is imperative to submit a completed application. Anything less is a waste of your time and hard work. Don't think you're going overboard if you end up "making your list and checking it much more than twice" – A funder may disqualify a proposal due to an oversight like forgetting to answer just one question, or neglecting to enter information into a single data field on an online application. This seemingly, simple oversight can result in your proposal being designated as incomplete.

You will be assured that you have included everything required by the funder if you list each and every item on your checklist (with a brief description of applicable details if needed). When you have finished writing your proposal, it is time to compile and collate your packet. Using the checklist that you developed during your thorough review of the application, verify that you have included a response to each question. Confirm that you have included all required attachments.

Once you're able to check off every set of parentheses ( ) or boxes [ ] on your checklist, you will be assured that your proposal includes everything requested by the funder.

Final Note Regarding E-apps

If you forget to enter information into a data field that is required to be completed, the system will usually respond with an auto-messages to indicate that one or more of the data fields is blank and requires the entry of information to proceed the next question. However, no e-app system will be able to determine if the information you entered within a data field is incomplete, which is why the use of a checklist is so important.

Grant Application Tracking Form

The **Grant Application Tracking Form** on the following page can be used to monitor the status of your grant writing activities. The information that you record here can be used to help you follow-up on proposals that are pending, as well as those for which you will receive rejection letters. Most importantly, you will have opportunity to record grants awarded as well. It is designed to:

- Record key information for each proposal submitted

- Provide a central recordkeeping system to update the status of all grant proposals submitted

- Serve as a tool to plan follow-up activities, including a schedule for the submission of additional grants

Unless the funder's instructions discourage direct contact, it is important to follow-up on every rejection to ask, "What would have made my proposal more competitive?" or "What can be done to strengthen my application in the future?". You can typically submit another application to the same funder in their next funding cycle or after one year (based on their guidelines).

You can recreate the form in a spreadsheet or columnar table format using readily available software.

Exercise 17 - Record Submitted Grant Application

Instructions: Use the **Grant Application Tracking Form** on the following page to record details about the completed proposal.

The Grantbuilder™ Grant Application Tracking & Status Form

Item #	Funder	Amount Requested	Purpose or Program	App Deadline	Date Submitted	Response Date	Amount Awarded	Follow-up Needed

Awardee Notification

Successful applicants are typically notified by a Grant Award Letter or an e-mail from the funding source. Government funders may send letters, distribute or post a list of the awardees on a website or send e-mail notifications. In some instances, a phone call or e-mail may precede other modes of notification to applicants. The written notification will contain instructions regarding the process to receive the grant funds.

- The award announcement may request that the applicant place a phone call to schedule an appointment to sign a contract or agreement <u>prior</u> to receiving grant funds.

- The award announcement may indicate a date and time that the applicant is expected to attend an orientation or other meeting to review and discuss the agreement prior to its signing.

- In the case of some corporate and foundation grants, a check for the total, or a portion of the total award may be enclosed in the envelope with the award notification. It will usually include instructions to review, sign and return an agreement as a condition of accepting the check.

- Considering that most funders always give less money than what was requested in the proposal, there may be an opportunity to "negotiate" changes in the program. (i.e. The applicant requested $50,000 to provide services to 200 clients. If the funder grants only $30,000, the client numbers and other program goals will need to be adjusted downward).

Declination Letters

Unfortunately, the world of grant writing does include an ample number of declines. These are usually sent in the form of a letter or e-mail. Don't ever take a "no" from a funder personally. You may have written a proposal that was competing with 75 other applicants for a total of only 10 available grants.

If the notification includes contact information and does not include a "Do Not Contact Us" notice from the funder, it is appropriate and also important to make an inquiry about what would have made your proposal more competitive. If they are willing to provide feedback, it may inform changes to make all of your future proposals stronger and more compelling for future submissions.

Always determine the date when you are eligible to submit another proposal to any funder that sends you a decline notification. Many funders have a policy of accepting only one proposal per agency, per 12-month period. This may be spelled out in their application guidelines. If not, this is an appropriate question to ask.

Program Reviews, Site Visits and Audits

All government grant awards entail some type of formal process to review programs that receive funding. The grantmaking agency and type of grant will dictate the timing and extent of the process. The process will be explained either in the original application materials, or it will be covered in the grant agreement. Some government funders have a post-award notification review or formal appeals process available to applicants who receive a "decline" notice.

Some funders may request a site visit after reviewing your proposal. Consider this a positive sign. It means that you have made it past the initial screening process that would have already resulted in a decline notification to some of the other applicants. At this stage, your proposal is among those still being considered.

Some funders will conduct a review during and/or after the term of the grant. It may involve a site visit to see your program in action. A funder has the right to review and audit all records that relate to programs and activities supported by their grant.

> An audit by a government funder often includes both a programmatic and fiscal audit. This type of fiscal audit is not the same as the annual audit conducted by a CPA.

A program review (sometimes called a "program audit") is not the same as the annual fiscal audit conducted by a CPA (certified public accountant) on the overall fiscal activities of the 501(c)(3) organization. The funder will assign one of its staff or other representatives to conduct the program review. In this instance the grantee will be responsible for gathering all requested documents and related information per the funder's request. The funder may also request assistance with coordinating interviews with the grantee's staff or clients. Aside from staff time, copies of documents and indirect expenses for the funder's temporary use of office space needed to conduct the review, the nonprofit does not occur any additional expenses for this process. However, the nonprofit does bare the responsibility and expense to hire a CPA to conduct an annual fiscal audit. Funds for the audit can be included in a grant request as long as the potential funding source allows support for this type of general operating expenses or administrative overhead expense.

The Payment Process

After a grantee has received an *announcement* or *notification* of a grant award, the grantee usually signs a contract or agreement that stipulates the terms of the grant. At this point, the payment process is initiated.

The agreement will cover both *programmatic* and *fiscal (financial)* aspects related to payment. *Programmatic* aspects deal with how the program or project is expected to operate, who it is intended to serve, where services are offered and who is responsible for complying with the grant agreement. *Fiscal* aspects deal with the billing process to receive payments, how the grantee is expected to account for the funds, and who has administrative responsibilities for complying with the grant agreement.

Funding sources typically disburse payment(s) to the grantees in one of two ways, as a full or partial advance upon awarding the grant, or as a reimbursement of funds that requires the grantee to submit an invoice. A summary of the methods is provided below:

- **Advance lump sum payment** of the entire award amount for one funding cycle (a funding cycle is typically one 12 month period, unless a shorter or longer period is specified by the funding source).

  Some foundation funders may enclose a check for the partial or full amount of the grant along with an award notification letter. Funders may require, or offer the grantee the option of receiving payment electronically. In this instance, the funder will request bank account information or provide an online link for the grantee to complete some type of registration process to receive grant funds.

- **Advance partial payment** made at the start of the funding cycle. The amounts and time increments will vary by funder. Example: A funder may provide a maximum advance payment totaling 10% to 25% of the total grant award.

  Partial payments typically require that the grantee submit a written request, in accordance with instructions provided by the funder.

The Payment Process (continued)

- **Reimbursement** for money spent from other sources by the grantee to operate the grant-funded program. This method usually requires the submission of an invoice with details of program expenditures, and sometimes originals or copies of receipts. You may be required to submit an invoice on a monthly, quarterly or other time increment stipulated in the grant agreement.

  This method is by far the most common method of disbursement for government grants. Therefore, it is imperative that the recipient have the financial resources in place to implement and maintain all expenses for the program during the initial start-up period; this is often stated as a requirement for certain government grants. A period of three months is usually recommended, as it provides ample time to account for the submission and approval of a monthly invoice, which is usually submitted between the 15th and final day of the month following the month of the operations and activities related to the grant. The invoice must undergo an approval process, which may take additional time, prior to the processing and disbursement of a payment to the grant awardee.

For some government grants, funds are not distributed until the entire program/project has been completed and a written report has been submitted. These types of reimbursement agreements are more likely for projects that have a limited and specific timeframe (i.e. arts grant awarded for a 60-day exhibit, annual one-day community health conference). Information regarding reimbursement after the completion of the project will be indicated in the application guidelines, or at some point during the award notification and grant agreement process.

Grant payments may be made monthly, quarterly, semiannually, annually or within any other timeframe stipulated in the agreement. A funder may disburse grant funds by check or electronic transfer, depending on their preference and grant agreement.

Reporting Requirements

Most funding sources require some type of report to determine that grant funds have been expended on the proposal they funded. Reports may be required monthly, quarterly, semiannually, annually or within a specific timeline after the end of the project.

The specific types of reports, number of reports, timeline for reports, content and format of reports, and the process for submitting reports will be stipulated in the contract or agreement.

The report(s) may include *narrative, statistical* and *financial* information.

- *Narrative* – description of program highlights and activities; may include references to special events, news articles, special community recognition, client success stories, etc.

- *Statistical* – provides information such as numbers of participants, "units of service", demographics of participants, etc.; also quantitative indicators to show the impact of the program (i.e. rate of reduction in overall average weight for participants in a program to combat obesity, increase in physical mobility for seniors enrolled in a physical therapy and fitness program)

- *Financial* – requires accounting information on the expenditure of funds that may include standard financial statements (i.e. operating statement showing revenue and expenses, balance sheet).

Some funders provide a financial reporting form that the grantee must fill in with information to indicate exactly how grant funds were spent. Backup documentation is sometimes required (i.e. receipts, copies of bank statements, cancelled checks, signed copies of contracts with consultants).

> *It is good practice to prepare and submit a final report on your program to the funder even if it is not required. This document is also useful for your internal program management purposes.*

Fine-Tuning Your Grant Writing Skills

Grant writing is a knowledge- and skill-based, art form that can be adapted to fit different programs and different funders. If you understand that rejection and declination letters are just a part of the landscape, you can learn not to take it personally. The only way to develop and refine your grant writing skills is to review and apply what you have learned thus far, then practice, practice, practice. Consider the following recommendations:

If you don't have a program that you've identified for writing a grant, you may want to consider volunteering to prepare one or more grants for a nonprofit agency or local school in your community to gain real-world experience. To start, it will be very helpful to spend time inside the agency as a volunteer. Many of these organizations have volunteer opportunities for time-limited, one-time projects, annual events and ongoing programs.

Serving as a volunteer will help you to become familiar with how the agency's mission and purpose aligns with their programs and services. This will also allow you to gain a better understanding of how the organization operates. Most importantly, you will have the opportunity to see the agency in action serving its clients. By gaining hands on experience as an insider, you will develop a better understanding of the agency. The depth and breadth of interacting in this manner can help you to tell the agency's story with more passion in the proposal, which will make it more compelling and competitive to a funder.

Once you're ready to roll up your sleeves and get started, consider joining the board of a local nonprofit organization and volunteer to work with the staff responsible for fundraising. Offer your services to assist with the agency's grant writing activities, including research to locate funding sources and/or preparing grant applications.

Participate in educational activities designed for nonprofit professionals. The more you learn about the operations of nonprofits, the more well-rounded you will become as a grantwriter. (See resources for nonprofits on pages 50-51 and 232-233)

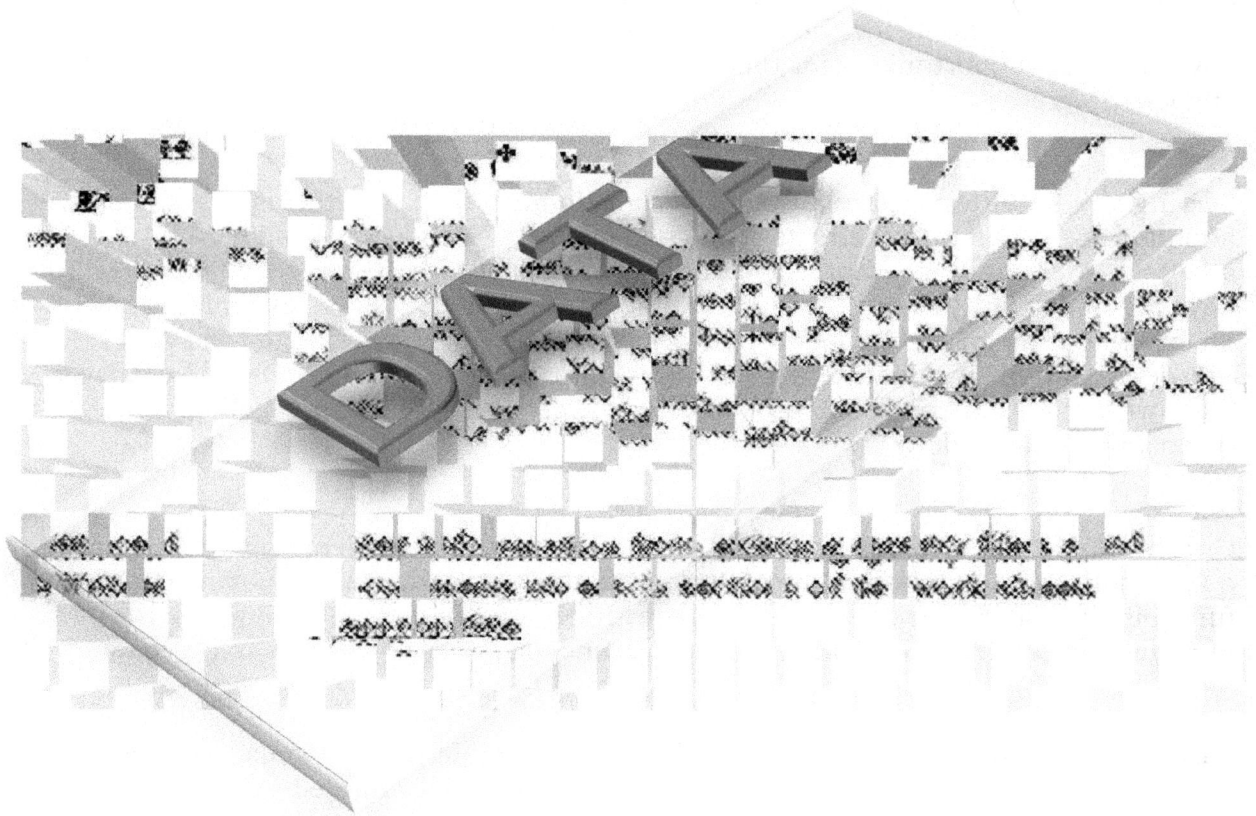

Part IX: Master Grant Data Worksheet

This section includes a set of forms designed for you to record all categories of information needed to complete all types of grant applications.

After completing this section, you will be able to:

- Compile a complete set of information for every category of information that may be required by any funding source

- Cut & paste sections to respond to questions on grant applications

- Complete grants applications faster with a system that makes it easy to locate, retrieve and edit response to questions

- Have a thorough understanding of each of the ten most common categories of information requested by funders for the agency and programs for which you're preparing grant proposals

As you proceed with the completion of exercises in this workbook, concurrently it is important to begin the process of collecting and recording information onto the **Master Grant Data Worksheet** in this section. If you will follow this recommendation, you will have all of the information needed to prepare any type of grant application by the time you complete this workbook.

Master Grant Data Worksheet

The Grantbuilder™ has developed this multi-page worksheet to make it easy to capture, record and organize all categories of information needed to prepare grant applications. This system reduces the time needed to review and update categories of information required by all funding sources.

The worksheet is designed with two columns. The left column includes instructions and prompts to help you recall or think of the most appropriate responses. The corresponding spaces in the right column will be used to record your responses, including notes for any follow-up required to complete a response. The worksheet can also be used as an interview tool to gather information from nonprofit managers, staff and others. Keep in mind that information may not be available to provide a response to every single prompt. Some questions won't relate to every program. However, it is important to address each question in each section to determine if you will be able to prepare a response. This will ensure that you will have all required information and documents readily available to prepare any type of grant application.

The completed worksheet will make the writing task more manageable by organizing the data in a convenient, easy-to-follow format. Pages at the end of the worksheet have sections with titles left blank. These can be used to record additional categories of information. The worksheet also makes it easy to add and edit additional information on an ongoing basis. Review the following tips:

Level of Experience	Tips to Complete Master Grant Data Worksheet
New Grant Writers	The use of bullet points is highly recommended to prepare brief responses. Later, you can return to fill-in additional details as you develop or gather information from existing files or other documents that contain relevant information.
Experienced Grant Writers	Enter information from existing agency files and documents into each section of the worksheet as appropriate.

Most data fields on the worksheet are formatted to accept data in narrative form. This makes it easier to highlight contiguous sections of text that you will need to "cut & paste" into data fields in online applications. This also applies to the preparation of drafts for hard copy applications. Follow the instructions below:

Step #1   Read the section heading, then review all of the questions and prompts in the left column for that section of the worksheet.

Step #2   Record your responses in the column to the right. You may use bullet points, take notes or "cut & paste" information from other grant documents or related sources. Remember, you are creating a worksheet with important information to add to your master grant template. Later, you will "cut & paste" your entries from this worksheet, into a wordprocessing document. This "working document" will be edited and finalized during the grant writing process.

Note: If the information is for a specific program, record the name of the program following the "**Program Name:**" heading at the top left of the page. Make additional copies of worksheet pages as needed to create a complete data set for each program.

Exercise 18 - Recording the Details to Write Your Proposal

Instructions: Record details for your program in each appropriate section on the following Master Grant Template Worksheet. This will provide all of the information needed to develop the narrative for any grant proposal that you prepare.

The Grantbuilder™ Master Grant Data Worksheet
Directory
(Page 1 of 2)

OVERALL AGENCY: Organizational Overview

PROGRAM SPECIFIC

OVERALL AGENCY	
ORGANIZATIONAL INFORMATION (Page 1 of 1)	
Agency's Legal Name	
AKA:	
Address:	
City	
State	
Zip Code	
Phone:	
Fax:	
Website:	
Facebook:	
Twitter:	
Other (list):	
Tax ID / EIN #:	
DUNS #:	
Other: Licenses/Certifications* (*list with relevant I.D. info)	
Additional Agency Info Special classifications, memberships, etc.	

OVERALL AGENCY	
ORGANIZATIONAL INFORMATION (Page 2 of 2)	
Primary Agency Contact	
Name, Job Title	
E-mail:	
Phone:	
Secondary Agency Contact	
Name, Job Title	
E-mail:	
Phone:	
Primary Grant Contact	
Name, Job Title:	
E-mail:	
Phone:	
Date Founded*:	
Date of IRS Tax Exemption: *The program may have existed prior to the nonprofit incorporation date & tax exempt status*	
Additional Location(s): *Address and type of location (i.e. administrative or program)*	

OVERALL AGENCY

BUDGET INFORMATION: Financial Profile of Overall Agency

Fill-in information for all items in the column to the right that apply to your agency/program.

Data should pertain to the current fiscal year.

Gather information from the organization's financial records to record dollar amounts (and the % of the total budget) for each type of funding included in your organization's budget.

Some funders require this type of detail. Those that do, usually provide a form with similar details as the one to the right. In any case, this detail will prove useful for any request for "line item" detail about an organization's revenue/income.

Prepare a brief summary of the categories of funding that support the budget for your organization to operate. It should be a concise narrative description of the "funding mix" reflected on the completed form above.

Note: If applicable, include a line item and reference to the support received from "inkind" contributions. Page 231 of the worksheet includes a form to document inkind donations.

Fiscal Year Starts (MM/DD): _____

Fiscal Year Ends (MM/DD): _____

Current Annual Agency Budget: $ _____

Type of Funding	Amount	%
Grants:		
Government	$ _____	_____ %
Foundation	$ _____	_____ %
Other Grants	$ _____	_____ %
Special Events:	$ _____	_____ %
Individual Donations:		%
Board Contributions	$ _____	_____ %
Individual Donors	$ _____	_____ %
Direct Mail/E-mail	$ _____	_____ %
Earned Income	$ _____	_____ %
Investment Income	$ _____	_____ %
Contracts	$ _____	_____ %
Endowment	$ _____	%
186Legacy/Planned Giving	$ _____	%
Other	$ _____	_____ %
Total:	$ _____	100 %*

*(Must equal 100%)

OVERALL AGENCY

ORGANIZATIONAL OVERVIEW: Mission Statement

Mission Statement	
Provide a summary description of the purpose.	
If applicable, include the following items:	
1) Values and/or Vision Statement	
2) Guiding Principles	

OVERALL AGENCY

ORGANIZATIONAL OVERVIEW: General Description

Note: It is recommended that you complete pages 189-201 <u>before</u> preparing a narrative for the General Description on this page.

<u>After</u> you complete the entire **Master Grant Data Worksheet,** you will have all of the information needed to prepare a summary overview of the organization, which should address the following questions:

What?
What does the organization do?

When? How long has the organization been in operation? Are there some activities that happen on an annual or ongoing basis?

Who?
Who is involved (who are the clients and who is providing services – i.e. background or qualifications of staff/volunteers)

Where? Location of organization's headquarters and where programs and services are provided.

How? Describe how the organization gets the support needed to operate (i.e. what sources?)

OVERALL AGENCY

ORGANIZATIONAL OVERVIEW: History

Historical Overview

Who started the organization?

Why was it started?

Describe the evolution of the agency, including highlights, accomplishments and challenges.

OVERALL AGENCY

ORGANIZATIONAL OVERVIEW: Staff Overview

How many FTE's? Special skills, licenses or certifications?

Provide a snapshot/profile of your current or proposed staffing for the overall agency: See example of list below:

- *1 f/t Director*

- *1 f/t Adm. Asst.*

- *3 p/t Outreach Workers*

- *1 p/t Counselor, M.A.*

- *1 p/t Driver*

Highlight significant accomplishments of staff, specifically as it relates to how their participation enhances your agency or program. Include a brief description of contributions that have had a positive impact on the agency.

Use the **Staff Roster** on page 226 to capture the level of detail requested by some funding sources.

OVERALL AGENCY

ORGANIZATIONAL OVERVIEW: Target Population

Who do you currently serve?

If the information is for a specific program, record the information on page 207. Prepare a separate sheet for each program.

Provide a general description of the target population(s) that your agency serves, overall.

Note: Use sheet on page 207 to prepare a profile of the target population for each program.

Total # clients served? _____

What % are low-income? _____ %

What criteria do you use to define low-income?
Federal poverty guidelines? Regional criteria? Etc.?

Demographic Profile:

Some of the most commonly requested categories are listed in the column to the right. However, some funders will label/group them differently. Each of the four categories to the right must total 100%.

Ethnicity		Gender	
_____%	African American	_____%	Male
_____%	Asian/PI	_____%	Female
_____%	Caucasian	_____%	Transgender
_____%	Hispanic	100%	Total
_____%	Native American		
_____%	Other		
100%	Total		

Age (category)		Education	
		_____%	High School Diploma/Equiv.
_____%	Infants	_____%	High School Dropout
_____%	Children	_____%	College Coursework
_____%	Young Adults	_____%	College Grad (BA/BS)
_____%	Adults	_____%	Graduate Degree
_____%	Adults (Seniors)	_____%	Post Graduate
100%	Total	100%	Total

*Asian, Pacific Islander

SUSTAINABILITY (1 of 3): Fundraising Plan for Overall Agency

Describe your fund development program:

What types of activities do you have planned or currently in place?

- *Grant writing?*
- *Sponsorships?*
- *Special Events?*
- *Program Income?*
- *Cause Marketing?*
- *Other?*

What is the status of your grant writing activities? Applications pending? Applications scheduled for submission? To which funders, for what purpose and for what amounts? (Use the **Grant Application Tracking & Status Form** on page 171 to track and update this information)

Highlight each of your most successful fundraising activities, including:

- Dollar amount(s) raised
- Percent of the total budget represented by each activity, and
- How these activities strengthen the organization's fundraising capacity

SUSTAINABILITY (2 of 3): Fundraising Plan for Overall Agency

What is the plan to raise funds for the agency's annual budget on an ongoing basis?	
Describe your agency's capacity to raise the funds needed, including: • *Background and expertise of fundraising staff* • *Existing resources (type of donor management software, significant inkind and volunteer support)* *Note: Include amounts raised per year, per activity, etc. for the current and most recently completed fiscal year.*	
What other resources do you currently have in place <u>or</u> have access to, to support the organization?	

SUSTAINABILITY (page 3 of 3): Fundraising Plan for Overall Agency

Does your organization operate fee-based programs or social enterprise activities that generate revenue?

If yes, describe each one, along with the total amount or percent of the program budget is raised from this revenue?

List any programs you operate that have the potential to generate revenue through fees collected from clients or service fees paid by a funding source, etc.*

*Indicate the program components most reasonable and likely to be developed and marketed to generate revenue?

What other resources will you pursue and when?

What is your board's contribution to, and involvement in fundraising?

BOARD INFORMATION (1 of 4): List of Board Members (Basic)

List of Board members*

The following format is recommended to prepare a basic board list. This format makes it easy to "cut & paste" into a hard copy proposal format <u>and</u> into online applications that do <u>not</u> require a separate entry for each board member into an individual data field.

Sample listing/entry:

Susan Jamejns, Ph.D.
Board Secretary*
Director of Operations
Kamway Industries
Los Angeles, CA
sjamejns@yahoo.com
(626) 123-4567

- *Insert line space*
- *Repeat format for next name*

*Indicate board officers and other formal roles as applicable (Pres., VP, Treasurer, Secretary; Committee Chair, etc.)

If applicable, it is appropriate to indicate "retired" along with a board member's former professional affiliation

BOARD INFORMATION (2 of 4): List of Board Members (Details)

In addition to preparing a list with basic information, it is important to gather some additional details on each board member that is routinely requested by some funders,* including:

• Mailing address

• Resume or Curriculum Vitae

• Board tenure

• Significant board contributions

• Professional accomplishments and/or affiliations that demonstrate the value they add to the agency

*Use the **Individual Board Member Profile Form on** page 227 to gather details for each member.

Note: Prepare the same information for each governing or advisory body (i.e. Advisory Board, Board of Regents)

BOARD INFORMATION (3 of 4): Participation

Total number of board seats?
(per agency's bylaws)

Total number of current board members?

What is the demographic profile of the board? (i.e. gender, ethnicity).

Do board members have a minimum requirement for annual personal fundraising or giving?*

If yes:
- What is the amount?*

- How many board members made a personal cash donation?

- What is the total amount donated by all board members?
  (*indicate amount for most recent fiscal year or specify the time period)

Schedule and frequency of board meetings?

Average number of board members that attend meetings?

BOARD INFORMATION (4 of 4): Additional Leadership Groups

List and provide a brief description of each internal leadership group affiliated with the agency (i.e. Advisory Board, Board of Governors, Corporate Advisory Committee)

Include any other pertinent information to demonstrate the strength of your board as a leadership group.

PROGRAM NAME:

PROGRAM DESCRIPTION: Overview

What is the purpose for the program?

If applicable, provide the mission statement for the specific program.

Is this a new program?
If not…

…How long has this program been in existence?

…What year did it start?

…Who started it?
(include appropriate response if program is new)

…Why was it started?
This relates to the "needs assessment" (Indicate if this is a new program)

…What resources did it take to get started and who provided them? (If this is a new program, indicate what is needed to get started)

PROGRAM NAME:

PROGRAM DESCRIPTION: Highlights and Accomplishments

List and describe the program's major accomplishments, successes and highlights. *(include dates if possible, exact or approximate)*

If this is a new program, describe what the program is designed to accomplish.

PROGRAM NAME:

PROGRAM OVERVIEW: Program Description (for proposed or existing program)

Program Description

Describe the program design, a list of major components and a brief description of activities.

Describe how the program will operate.

What is the service delivery area? Where will the services be provided? (region, locations, etc.)

PROGRAM NAME:
GOALS & OBJECTIVES

Indicate the goals and objectives for the proposed program.

The list of goals and objectives must include some quantitative outcomes (i.e. can be measured in units and should be developed with specific timelines in mind)

Examples include:

For a counseling center, number of clients and number of hours of counseling

For an after-school program, number of students, families and/or classrooms served

For a food pantry, number of families and/or bags of groceries distributed

For an adolescent conflict resolution program, anticipated (%) reduction in number of altercations, trips to principal's office at school, etc.

Note: Deliverables and outcomes from this worksheet will be used to prepare workplans for the respective program.

PROGRAM NAME:

TIMELINE & WORKPLAN

How long will it take to accomplish the goals and objectives?	
Indicate if this is a one-year or multi-year program.	
Note: A timeline should be prepared for each 12-month interval. A separate form will be used to prepare a detailed timeline or Scope of Work for each program proposed for funding.	
What is the timeline for the program? What is the projected schedule to implement key components?	
Indicate the projected milestones to be accomplished within specific timelines (i.e. by certain months, quarters or other dates)	

PROGRAM NAME:

PROGRAM DESCRIPTION: Location(s) for Program Activities

Where will activities take place?

One site or multi-site?

Why have you chosen the designated site(s) for the program or service?

What makes it a good location?

Satellite programs?

Will you rent space at the satellite location or will it be donated?

Will you collaborate with another organization to provide your program at their facility?

PROGRAM NAME:

PROGRAM BUDGET

Program Budget

Step 1:
As a starting point, refer to the **Program Design Worksheet** that you prepared for your program.

Step 2:
Use this worksheet section to prepare a projected summary "ballpark" budget with info from Step 1 above.

Step 3:
The detailed budget can be prepared using the Budget Worksheets (see pages 138-143)

Step 4:
Use this worksheet space to develop a list of any special equipment, professional licensing fees or other items that will be required for your program.* This information will be used later to conduct the research needed to prepare the detailed budget referenced above in Step 3.

*(*i.e. x-ray machine for a clinic, installation of special floor for a dance studio, fishing gear for a camping program)*

Summary Budget

Personnel: $ _____
(Salary/Wages & Benefits)

Operating Expenses: $ _____

Total: $ _____

Admin. Overhead:* $ _____
(_____% of **Total**)

Total Budget: $ _____

Enter your agency's rate for administrative overhead. A rate of 10% to 12% is recommended if you do not have an established rate.

Use the area below for notes related to your budget if needed:

PROGRAM NAME:

TARGET POPULATION

If this is a current program, whom does it serve? If this is a new program, describe the intended audience. *This is the group that will derive the greatest benefit from the program.*

Primary participants
What is the demographic profile?
- *Gender*
- *Age range*
- *Income level*
- *Education level*

Who are they?
- *Adults*
- *Families*
- *Seniors*
- *Students K-12*
- *Children*
- *Foster youth*
- *LGBT*
- *Previously incarcerated*
- *General population*

Where are they?
(Region, community, zip codes, etc. Later, this information can also be used to develop your outreach plan to recruit and enroll clients)

PROGRAM NAME:

TARGET POPULATION: Program-Specific

List any other unique characteristics or needs of the target population?	
Total # of unduplicated clients served (or to be served) in a one-year period.	_____
What % are low-income?	_____%
What criteria do you use to define low-income? *Federal poverty guidelines? Regional criteria? Etc.?*	

Demographic profile of clients for this program:

Some of the most commonly requested categories are listed in the column to the right. However, some funders will label/group them differently. Each of the four categories to the right must total 100%.

Ethnicity		**Gender**	
_____%	African American	_____%	Male
_____%	Asian/PI*	_____%	Female
_____%	Caucasian	_____%	Transgender
_____%	Hispanic	100 %	**Total**
_____%	Native American		
_____%	Other		
100%	**Total**		

		Education	
		_____%	High School Diploma/Equiv.
Age (category)		_____%	High School Dropout
_____%	Infants	_____%	College Coursework
_____%	Children	_____%	College Grad (BA/BS)
_____%	Young Adults	_____%	Graduate Degree
_____%	Adults	_____%	Post Graduate
_____%	Adults (Seniors)	100%	**Total**
100%	**Total**		

*Asian, Pacific Islander

Secondary participants

Indicate others who may benefit, although they aren't directly involved.

(Example: a senior day care program is of benefit to the relatives or caregivers who care for seniors)

PROGRAM NAME:

NEEDS ASSESSMENT (1 of 2)

Note: This section will be used to highlight what will be improved or corrected by the program. However, a formal needs assessment is usually written with a focus on defining and describing the problem that will be addressed by the program.

How have you determined that this program is needed?

Personal observation or experience?

Formal assessment process? (conducted by internal means or by third-party)

- *Focus groups*
- *Program evaluations*
- *Client surveys*

What sources provided this information?

What studies, articles or other independent, third-party sources indicate a need for this program?

In addition to any well-known, landmark studies, be sure to include some data compiled within the past year (with the references cited).

PROGRAM NAME:

NEEDS ASSESSMENT (2 of 2)

Have you gathered feedback from persons who have indicated a need for or an interest in this program?

If yes…

…Who are they?

…What is their feedback?

If not, identify people and sources likely to have useful input about the need or ideas about solutions

…Why do the participants need the program?

…Why does the community need the program?

PROGRAM NAME:

COMPETITION, COLLABORATIONS & PARTNERSHIPS

What programs offer the same, or similar services in the community?

Who is your competition?

Why is your program needed if there are similar programs?

Are other programs unable to accommodate the number of clients who need services?

Does your program provide something different?

Will your program serve a different target population?

Do you collaborate or have plans to collaborate with other programs? If yes, which ones and for what types of activities?

If applicable, describe your history of collaborations with other organizations and programs.

Use the **Collaborations & Partnerships Worksheet** on page 228 to record additional details.

PROGRAM NAME:

PROGRAM DESCRIPTION: Timeline/Work Plan - Duration and Scheduling

What is the proposed scheduling for program activities?

How often?

Daily, weekly, monthly, after school, evenings, weekends, etc.?

Hours, days, weeks, etc.?

What is the duration of the program?

If applicable, indicate the plan for holiday breaks, seasonal interruptions, etc.

(Example: A 12-week program scheduled to start in mid-October should account for "down time" during the holiday season to account for a scheduled break, or the anticipated temporary decrease in participation)

PROGRAM NAME:

PROGRAM DESCRIPTION: Outreach & Marketing (1 of 2)

How will you reach your target audience with information about the program?

How will you notify the community of your services?

List each type of tool and/or activity that you plan to use along with a brief description of <u>how</u> you plan to use it.

For example:
- *Social media (digital)*
- *Flyers*
- *Mailings*
- *Community events*
- *Advertising**

*Will you spend money on advertising or social media tools? If so, which ones? Internet, print, radio, TV, billboards, etc.

Include a summary of the historical and/or current use, including which have been the most effective

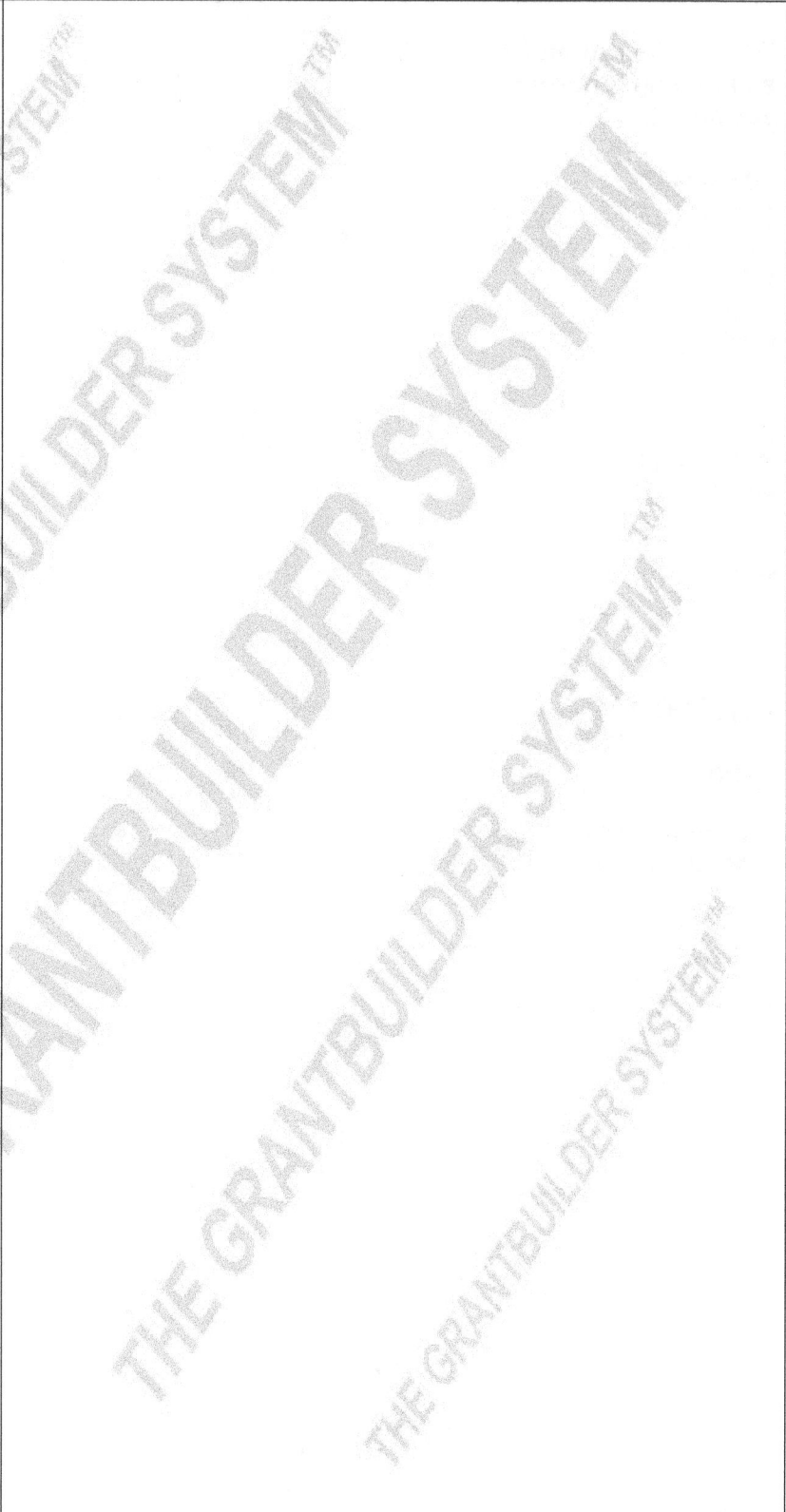

PROGRAM NAME:	
PROGRAM DESCRIPTION: Outreach & Marketing (2 of 2)	
Outreach & Marketing Will other organizations or groups (collaborators) be involved in your outreach activities? *If yes, which ones? Who are they? What role will they play?* Who is responsible for developing your outreach plan and materials? Who will coordinate and implement your outreach plan? What are their qualifications?	

PROGRAM NAME:

PROGRAM DESCRIPTION: Staffing – Paid Personnel

Important Note: It is imperative to establish a policy and written plan for a ***third-party* screening process*** for all paid staff, volunteers and consultants who will be working with minors (clients under the age of 18 years old) or others unable to assume responsibility for themselves legally (i.e. mentally disabled, medically incapacitated).

Staffing - Paid Personnel

List each staff or key function that is needed to operate the program.

Indicate if these are current positions, new job classifications and/or positions for this program.

If new positions, provide the proposed job title(s) and a succinct description of the role(s) & responsibilities

For each position, indicate:
- Full-time?
- Part-time?
- Educational standards?
- Special certification or licensing requirements?

What is your policy for third-party screening of all paid personnel?

*For background checks, contact your local law enforcement office for information on the process in your area.

PROGRAM NAME:

PROGRAM DESCRIPTION: Staffing – Volunteers

Important Note: It is imperative to establish a policy and written plan for a ***third-party* screening** *process* for all paid staff, volunteers and consultants who will be working with minors (clients under the age of 18 years old) or others unable to assume responsibility for themselves legally (i.e. mentally disabled, medically incapacitated).

Staffing – Volunteers
If you plan to use volunteers, indicate what roles they will play? Indicate key function and/or job titles?

What is your plan for:

- Recruitment?
- Training?
- Ongoing supervision and support?
- Recognition?

What is your policy for third-party screening of all volunteer personnel?

*For background checks, contact your local law enforcement office for information on the process in your area.

PROGRAM NAME:

PROGRAM DESCRIPTION: Staffing – Paid Consultants & Independent Contractors

Important Note: It is imperative to establish a policy and written plan for a ***third-party* screening process*** for all paid staff, volunteers and consultants who will be working with minors (clients under the age of 18 years old) or others unable to assume responsibility for themselves legally (i.e. mentally disabled, medically incapacitated).

Staffing – Paid Consultants & Independent Contractors

If you plan to use consultants, indicate what roles they will play? Indicate key function and/or job titles?

For each position, indicate:
- Full-time?
- Part-time?
- Educational standards?
- Special certification or licensing requirements?

What is your policy for third-party screening of consultants and contractors who may provide direct services or interact with your agency's clients?

*For background checks, contact your local law enforcement office for information on the process in your area.

PROGRAM NAME:

PROGRAM DESCRIPTION: Facility

Describe the location, size and features that make the venue(s) appropriate for existing and/or proposed program(s) *Meeting rooms? Playground for children's program? Etc.?* *Does the agency rent, lease or own the property?* **Parking** *Sufficient? Onsite? Adjacent? Free?* **Public Transportation** *Important for programs that serve seniors, disabled or low-income clients.* **ADA Accessible** *For individuals with physical limitations? (Is the site in compliance with standards under the **ADA**, American Disabilities Act)?* **Equipment** *(related to the facility, security system, exterior signage, etc.)* **Fixtures and Furnishings** *(special features that enhance program operations)*	

PROGRAM NAME:

PROGRAM DESCRIPTION: Equipment & Supplies – Direct Services for Program Participants

Use this section to prepare the list of resources that will be used by:

1) Program participants (i.e. clients) and
2) Staff that provide direct services to clients

Equipment
List and describe use of equipment that may be unique to the program

Example: video editing software for a youth multimedia project, sports equipment for an athletics program.

Supplies & Materials
Include supplies that will be used by program participants.

Example: Painting supplies for a construction trades program, latex gloves for a medical assistant program, etc.

Consider the quantity of supplies that will be consumed. Use the information to estimate the expenses for these items.

Software
Include software purchase and/or upgrade and applicable licensing fees

Professional Services
Include other expenses needed to support the program *(i.e. monthly internet subscriptions, registration fees for professional trainings)*

Licenses & Permits
Include fees for all applicable licenses, etc. required for the program to operate

Other
Include other resources needed to operate the program. Identify resources that will be provided through inkind contributions.

PROGRAM NAME:

PROGRAM DESCRIPTION: Equipment & Supplies – Administration

Use the section to prepare the list of resources that will be used by staff for the *administrative operations** needed to support the program.

*These are items that will be used by staff who have little or no involvement in providing direct services.

Example: Staff with little to no involvement in providing direct services to clients, however they provide support to the program on an ongoing or interim basis (i.e. I.T. staff, Accounting Manager, Director of Development, Grant Writer)

Example: New accounting software/service needed to manage donor information for fundraising that supports every program in the organization.

Include a list of major items and/or categories of everything needed to set-up and support the administrative functions of the program

- Equipment
- Supplies & Materials
- Software
- Professional Services
- Licenses or Permits
- Other

PROGRAM NAME:	
EVALUATION	
Discuss the (intended or actual) impact of the program and how your organization defines "success" for each program. How do you plan to measure the progress and success of the program? The measurements should be tied to the *units of service* or *outcomes* included in the **Goals and Objectives** section on page 202. *What method(s) will be used?* *What tool(s) will be used?* Who is responsible for the evaluation and what are their qualifications? *Internal evaluation process by staff?* *Third-party consultant?*	

PROGRAM NAME:

SUSTAINABILITY (Part 1 of 2)

What resources do you currently have to support this program? If applicable, indicate the dollar amount and list/describe the source(s) of support

- Current funding?
- Current in-kind resources?

Current Funding Sources   Amount

_____ $_____
_____ $_____
_____ $_____
_____ $_____
_____ $_____
Total Funding Support for Program: $_____

Current Inkind Support
(Describe specific goods or services provided)

_____ $_____
_____ $_____
_____ $_____
_____ $_____
_____ $_____
Total Inkind Support for Program: $_____
Combined Totals (Funding + Inkind): $_____

Have you submitted other grant applications for this program? If so, to whom and for what amount?

What other resources will you pursue and when?

Describe any current or recent (w/in prior year) fundraising activities specific to this program. If no information is available, describe what is proposed for the current year and/or for this new program.

PROGRAM NAME:

SUSTAINABILITY (Part 2 of 2)

What is the plan to maintain the program <u>after</u> the funding cycle covered by this grant application?

What other resources do you have to continue the program?

Does this program generate revenue <u>or</u> does this program have the potential to generate revenue through fees collected from clients, service fees paid by a funding source, etc.? If so, what amount or percent of the program budget is raised from this revenue?

Do you have any individual donors or other sources that provide funding for this specific program?

Does this program have any components that can be developed and marketed for sale to generate revenue?

Describe successful fundraising activities specific to this program.

PROGRAM NAME:

OTHER: [   ]

Place an appropriate heading in the data field above. List and address any additional items requested in the application and/or other information that is important or helpful to include. Use the left column to list key items, and use the corresponding section to the right to record applicable details. Save/Create additional copies of this page as needed.

List of Items	Description or Details

PROGRAM NAME:

OTHER: [   ]

Place an appropriate heading in the data field above. List and address any additional items requested in the application and/or other information that is important or helpful to include. Use the left column to list key items, and use the corresponding section to the right to record applicable details. Save/Create additional copies of this page as needed.

List of Items	Description or Details

List of Items	Description or Details

PROGRAM NAME:

OTHER: [   ]

Place an appropriate heading in the data field above. List and address any additional items requested in the application and/or other information that is important or helpful to include. Use the left column to list key items, and use the corresponding section to the right to record applicable details. Save/Create additional copies of this page as needed.

List of Items	Description or Details
List of Items	**Description or Details**
List of Items	**Description or Details**

Staff Roster

#	Staff Name	Job Title	FTE	M/F	Anniv. Date	Other

Individual Board Member Profile

Updated as of ____/____/____

(make copies as needed)

Personal Contact Information	
Name:	If board officer or other official role, indicate position:
Mailing Address:	E-mail:
Phone – A:	Phone - A:

Professional Affiliation		
Occupation/Job Title (indicate if retired):		
Company:		**Demographic Profile**
City & State:		( ) M ( ) F Ethnicity:
Resume or curriculum vitae received on ____/____/____		( ) Youth ( ) Low-income Other:
Education - *list degree(s)/school(s)*:		
Professional licensure/certification:		
List or briefly describe significant contributions to the agency:		

Notes:

Roster of Collaborators and Community Partnerships

(make copies as needed)

#	Name of Organization or Community Group **and** Address	Contact Person/Info	Brief Description of Collaboration

Roster of Most Commonly Requested Attachments

Instructions: Use this form to create a directory listing of the grant attachments that you will need to retrieve/copy on a regular basis. Use the first column to record the date (MM/YR) of the most recent document. Use the two right columns to record the names and locations of the files. A blank copy of this form is provided on the following page to list additional attachments.

Doc Date	Attachment	Digital Filename & location	Hardcopy Filename & Location
	IRS 501(c)(3) Determination Letter		
	Annual Agency Budget(s)		
	IRS 990: (Tax) Return of Organization Exempt from Income Tax		
	Audited Financial Statements aka "Audit"		
	Board List		
	Letter(s) of Support Specific to program and/or grant request		
	Agency's brochure, newsletter or similar material		
	Proof of liability insurance		
	Workers' Compensation Insurance		
	Licensing or Certification		
	Funding History		
	(Financial) Operating Statements		
	IRS W-9 Form: Request for Taxpayer ID Number and Certification		
	State Nonprofit Certificate		

Roster of Most Commonly Requested Attachments

Use this page to record additional documents that you may need to submit with proposals on a routine basis.

Doc Date	Attachment	Digital Filename & location	Hardcopy Filename & Location

Notes:

[ ] OVERALL AGENCY   [ ] SPECIFIC PROGRAM:

BUDGET INFORMATION: Valuation of Volunteer & Inkind Contributions

Volunteer Contributions (Time/Talent):

Step 1: List appropriate job title(s) <u>or</u> type of service that describes the inkind contribution. (If a person or company was being paid to perform the task, what is an appropriate job title?)

Examples:
- **Graphic Designer** *prepares the agency's monthly newsletter as inkind*
- *Three volunteers (each) work a four-hour shift once a week as* **Drivers** *to deliver meals to homebound seniors*
- *Local restaurant donates* **Food/Catering** *for agency's annual fundraiser*

Step 2: List inkind contributions of goods (tangible items) by category or list individual items of significant value.

Examples:
- **Office Supplies** *donated to the agency throughout the year (enter one total)*
- *Refrigerator donated for the staff lounge*

Step 3: Calculate and record an amount on the corresponding "$" **Value** line reflecting an amount that the organizations would have to pay to secure the same quality, level and frequency of the service provided.

Note: Volunteer time by board members to perform their regular duties should <u>not</u> be listed. However, any contribution of goods or professional services beyond regular board duties should be recorded.

Role, Function or Inkind Contribution	Dollar/Market Value of Services (Annual)
	$
	$
	$
	$
	$
	$
	$
	$
	$
	$
	$
	$
	$
	$
Total Inkind Contributions:	$

<u>Additional Notes Regarding Inkind Donations</u>

231

The Center for Grant Writing™ (TCG)

"Interactive, hands-on training in the art of grant writing"

The Center for Grant writing (TCG) is an online resource that provide training, mentoring and resources to equip individuals and organizations with knowledge and skills for success in securing grant funds from government, foundation and corporate sources. Programs, publications and services for the Center are developed and marketed under The Grantbuilder™ brand.

Workshops and professional development programs are conducted online and in traditional, classroom formats with collaborating community partners throughout the U.S. Our online mentoring program provides ongoing support to TCG participants.

All TCG instructors and mentors have extensive grantmaking experience and a demonstrated track record of success preparing applications and proposals that have resulted in grant awards for the following types of organizations:

·   Community-based nonprofits

·   Public institutions, including schools, libraries, hospitals and community clinics

·   Faith-based organizations

·   Government offices and agencies, including health, law enforcement, etc.

TCG offers pre-packaged and customized workshops and fund development courses tailored to address the needs of nonprofit board members, staff and volunteers.

We also serve as a referral source for organizations seeking professional grant writing consulting services.

For more information, visit www.TheGrantBuilder.com

Contact Information:
The Grantbuilder/TCG
710 S. Myrtle Avenue #284
Monrovia, CA 91016
info@thegrantbuilder.com

Founded by La Quetta M. Shamblee

Additional Resources for Grant Writing and Nonprofit Development

Community Foundations
This website is a resource for professional advisors, donors and media representatives.
www.communityfoundations.net

Fiscal Sponsor Directory
This website was established by the San Francisco Study Center to help connect community projects with fiscal sponsors. It also provides a platform to foster an understanding of fiscal sponsorship and its impact on the nonprofit sector.
www.fiscalsponsordirectory.org

Grants.gov
The U.S. Department of Health and Human Services manages Grants.gov, the website to locate and review the listing of all grants offered by the federal government.
http://grants.gov/

GuideStar USA, Inc.
Guidestar is a nonprofit organization that specializing in reporting on nonprofits in the U.S. They maintain one of the largest databases of financial information on nonprofit organizations. As of 2010, they had more than five million IRS forms on 1.9 million nonprofit organizations.
www.guidestar.com

Internal Revenue Service (IRS)
The IRS is the U.S. government agency responsible for tax collection and tax law enforcement. Their website includes information and forms for the 501(c)(3) application process, as well as downloadable copies and instructions to complete the the Form 990 (Return of Organization Exempt From Income Tax).
www.irs.gov

The National Network of Fiscal Sponsors
The National Network of Fiscal Sponsors improves the practice of fiscal sponsorship and promotes its value to society. This website is a good resource for information on fiscal sponsorships.
www.tides.org/community/networks-partners/nnfs/

Nolo
Nolo, Inc. has been publishing do-it-yourself legal guides since 1971, including resources for establishing a nonprofit.
www.nolo.com

The Chronicle of Philanthropy
Based in Washington, D.C., this publication covers the nonprofit world and is published 18 times a year, with daily updates to its website. It is a valuable resource for nonprofit leaders, foundation executives, fundraisers and others involved in working with or supporting charitable organizations.
www.philanthrophy.com

Index

ABOUT THE AUTHOR

La Quetta Shamblee has extensive hands-on experience in the nonprofit sector, including grants administration and contracts management. Her fund development and grant writing talents have resulted in millions in grants and sponsorships for community programs. She has managed multi-disciplinary staff and grant-funded programs at some of the largest HIV/AIDS organizations in Southern California. She served as the financial administrator for Los Angeles County's second largest HIV outpatient clinic, Deputy Director for Caring for Babies with AIDS and Director of Programs and Services for AIDS Service Center in Pasadena, CA. She also served as the Director of Development for one of the largest, regional multi-service agencies for low-income residents in the San Gabriel Valley region of the most populated county in the nation (Los Angeles County).

First 5 LA (Los Angeles County's Proposition 10 Commission) retained her services to conduct the first programmatic review of their largest single contract, a $584M, five-year agreement with Los Angeles Universal Preschool (LAUP). She has served on grant review panels for health, arts and culture and workforce development programs for government and foundation funders. She has also written RFP/RFA packets and coordinated the grantmaking process for government-funded projects, including an oral health initiative for services at community dental clinics. The project was a collaborative funding project between L.A. Care Health Plan and First 5 LA. She coordinated a similar process for a regional job placement program funded by the American Recovery and Reinvestment Act (ARRA aka "federal stimulus funds") for Foothill Unity Center, a federally designated Community Action Agencies in Los Angeles County.

She is an instructor for UCLA Extension in the Nonprofit Management and Fundraising Program. She has also designed customized curriculum and instructed courses for their organizational clients, including a certificate course in Federal Grants Management for staff at the Port of Long Beach. Her expertise has also been applied to the development of the Management module included in the Fundraising Certificate program that is designed to prepare UNEX students for the Certified Fund Raising Executive (CFRE) examination.

As the founder and executive director of The Instrumental Women Project (IWP), she has hands-on experience with launching and growing a grassroots arts organization. She secured co-production grants from the Los Angeles County Arts Commission for eight consecutive years to produce IWP's critically-acclaimed *Lady Jazz*™ Concert Series as part of the Ford Amphitheatre's Summer Season. This all-woman showcase of accomplished jazz instrumentalists has received numerous commendations.

Ms. Shamblee received her B.A. in Management from Pacific Christian College and an M.B.A. from Azusa Pacific University. She resides in the San Gabriel Valley region of Southern California.

www.ingramcontent.com/pod-product-compliance
Lightning Source LLC
Chambersburg PA
CBHW080416270326
41929CB00018B/3053